FROM Albariño TO Torrontés

FLAVORS, PAIRINGS, AND
PERSONALITIES OF THE WORLD'S MOST
UNDERRATED WINES

SHEA SANDERSON

To request permissions, email: contact@nouveaupress.com

ISBN: 978-1-7356753-2-9 (paperback)
ISBN : 978-1-7356753-3-6 (e-book)

First Edition: February 2021.

Edited by Nicky Guerreiro
Typesetting by Derek Murphy
Book and Cover design by Shea Sanderson

Published by Nouveau Press in the United States of America.
www.nouveaupress.com
For author info, visit www.sheasanderson.com

For Ashley – my first and forever wine-loving partner in crime.

CONTENTS

INTRODUCTION

WHEN IT COMES TO LEARNING about wine, many people wonder "why even make the effort?" After all, embarking on a wine tasting journey is not unlike pursuing an unpaid internship. The costs involved are way more than you had originally thought, you only get paid in experience, and you're not entirely sure how it'll help you become a better person. On the flip side, tasting journeys are fun, your boss is wine, and you get as much time off as you want. Why get involved, you ask? Because eventually, the world of wine becomes too intriguing to pass up.

Opening just one special bottle can change your entire view on wine. Suddenly, tasting becomes more than just an excuse to imbibe. It's a chance to explore, evaluate, and even open doors that you might have previously closed. I mean, one minute you're side-eyeing a $5 box of Zinfandel, wondering how anyone could deign to drink the stuff. The next you're raving on and on about how amazing a bottle of old vine Lodi Zinfandel is. I'm telling you; one taste can completely change how you approach all future bottles.

Once you get to that point, the point of no return, the world of wine becomes your kingdom. Everything the light touches becomes yours to explore. And much like Simba in *The Lion King*, you won't just stick to the territories you're familiar with. Eventually, you'll find yourself intrigued by what lies beyond.

Here, at the outer edges of the wine aisle, the bottom of the wine list, and the products of lesser-known vineyards, is where this book takes place. I like to call this outer periphery "Page Two." Attempting to reach the top of the wine world, both in terms of popularity and consumer demand, is like trying to rank on the first page of Google. It's really, really difficult. Borderline impossible. But that doesn't mean the second page of results is devoid of value. Especially when you've already tried everything on page one, and you want more. So here we are: page two.

These are the wines you've encountered in passing, whether while perusing the wine aisle or scanning a hard-tointerpret wine list at a restaurant. Or maybe you stumbled on an article arguing that Grüner Veltliner is the next Sauv Blanc (very likely), or how Lambrusco is making a comeback (I doubt it), and you wanted to find out more. I mean, let's face it, how can anyone keep up with all the wine varieties available? There are thousands (yes, thousands) of different wines; it's easy to get overwhelmed. I, for one, completely gave up on learning about wine for years for the exact same reason. But that won't happen with you, friend. This book, my second, will illuminate the world of underrated wines, leaving you well-equipped to move beyond the basics.

For those of you who have already journeyed with me in my first book, *From Cabernet to Zinfandel*, you know what to expect from me. But if you're new here, allow me to manage your expectations. After years of frustration, I developed a system for learning about and enjoying wine that works. It's easy, casual, and requires no one to get a WSET certification. Knowing that others have struggled or are struggling with their own wine education, I wanted to share what I've learned. I'm not a wine expert, or a critic, or a sommelier—I'm a normal human being with no credentials who found a way to engage with wine that was natural, easy, and helped me think about what I liked and when I'd drink it. I wholeheartedly expect you, my reader, to take this book and find your own way. My opinions are not gospel, but if I can help you approach wine in a way that works for you, then I've done my job. Now let's unpack this book so you'll know what to expect.

Each wine has its own profile and was hand-selected by your host, me, based on vineyard plantings and perceived popularity. With this book, I chose just outside of the top 25 varietals (I include the top 25 in *FCTZ*). I introduce each wine with pertinent background information including but not limited to its alter egos (regional name differences) and any dinner party facts that make the wine fun and interesting to talk about. Because let's be honest, wine can get really boring, really fast. When applicable, I also list the French regions and, more specifically, appellations where that wine can be found. You know, since the French refuse to budge on making their labels easy-to-read for the masses.

Following the introduction, I do a tasting. I choose a bottle based on little more than budget (most under $20) and region (I only choose bottles from the most notable regions that produce that particular wine). Here you'll get a description of the wine's flavors, structure (acid and tannin), and overall sensory experience. If the wine feels like it's taking a nap in your mouth because it's so full-bodied, I'll tell you. If it fizzes on the palate like Welch's sparkling grape juice, I'll tell you that too.

Finally, there's the "In the Wild" section—a section devoted to making the wine fit into your life. I use this section in one of two ways: to give the wine a personality so you can know which bottle will match the vibe you're going for, or to offer you a scenario in which this wine would pair perfectly. Food and wine pairings are well-handled on the internet and elsewhere. But here, here is where you get the wine recommendations for a first date that you're cooking for, a children's birthday party, and those days when you're too lazy to cook for yourself but you know you have to. It's fun, it's edgy, and it's completely up to you to take my word for it. But it will give you some idea which wine to pick for various moods and situations.

When all is said and done, I hope you walk away even more confident about wine and how to choose, taste, and describe it. I hope you feel armed and excited to scour the outer edges of the wine aisle, without being stymied or confused. And most importantly, I hope you enjoy yourself. Open up a bottle, discuss it with your friends, and bask in the glory of 25 more of the world's wines under your belt. After all, the world of wine is too intriguing to pass up, so here's to getting you even further.

Now, let's drink!

WHITE WINES & GRAPES

" 'I am not sure I trust you.' 'You can trust me with your life, My King.' 'But not with my wine, obviously. Give it back.' " – Megan Whalen Turner, The King of Attolia

ALBARIÑO

IN TERMS OF POPULARITY AMONGST Spanish whites, Albariño leads by a mile. And yet, when choosing a crisp white wine, people seem to forget about it. It can't be because it's new on the scene; Albariño vines have been growing for 300 years! And we know it can't be because people don't love it. August 1st is "Albariño Day," and wines don't get their own holidays for no reason. So why doesn't Albariño regularly crack the top five of white wines purchased? If it's because no one talks it up enough, then allow me to get the ball rolling.

Albariño immediately teaches you a thing or two about white wines, things you'll only read about until you experience them firsthand. For example, a select few white wines taste like saline (or saltwater), Albariño being one of the more well-known varieties to do so. I don't know about you, but learning that white wine can pack notes of salt blew my wine-obsessed mind. How am I supposed to believe that while I'm looking for tropical, stone, or citrus fruit flavors, I could stumble upon notes of *salt?* Oh, right—because of the effects of growing environments.

On the list of things I care about when choosing wines, knowing the hill or valley a grape has grown on always comes in second-to-last, just behind the popularity of the varietal. Growing environments have always been boring and, to me, irrelevant. At least they *were,* until I tasted my first Albariño and came face to face with the enigmatic note of saline. Sure, I had heard the rumors that some white wines had notes of salt, but I never really bought it. I was unconvinced that I would ever noticeably taste salt in a wine. It was too absurd to even entertain. But once I had that first sip, I was no longer a skeptic. I had to know why and how this contradictory flavor could naturally come about. And wouldn't you know it, the flavor had everything to do with where it was growing—right along the Atlantic coast of northwest Spain.

Turns out, that constant ocean breeze can really do wonders for a tiny grape like Albariño. All that sea air permeates the grapes, day in and day out, for months. No wonder saline is a distinctive flavor. The grape is inhaling that salty oceanic breeze every day until it's harvested. Mystery solved and lesson learned. Growing environments absolutely affect how your wine tastes. Which is why Albariño deserves to be sought after. Sure, Pinot Grigio is lean and crisp and Sauvignon Blanc is herby and leafy. But Albariño is *salty*. It's mythical until you taste it. And if you're anything like me, it's the wine teacher you never knew you needed.

THE TASTING

THE BOTTLE: *Adega Pazos de Lusco Albariño 2018. Galicia, Spain. $20.*

At first glance, this Albariño seems to be just like any other light white wine. It's straw-colored, much like a dry Riesling or Muscadet, and smells like grapefruit, beeswax, and apricot. Nothing out of sorts upon the first impression. A run of the mill, light, crisp, dry white wine. Until you taste it, of course.

Initially, this Pazos de Luscos tastes like honeydew, white nectarine, and a lick of lemon pith. The fruit lands first, allowing for the mouth-puckering acidity to quickly take over. Should you enjoy it at ice-cold temperatures, the acid will coat your entire mouth. But the finish is where Albariño sets itself apart.

The notoriously enigmatic flavor of saline brings up the rear. It's like licking a salt rock and, surprisingly enough, *adds* to the refreshing nature of the wine. To enjoy melon and nectarine wrapped up in lemony citrus is enough on its own. But to find saltiness pouring out from the front of your palate is enough to take anyone by surprise. The biggest surprise for me is that this seawater note is utterly delicious in the context of this wine.

So, I guess the rumors turned out to be true: coastal white wines like Albariño prove that salt doesn't just belong in your dinner. It can easily belong in your wine, too.

IN THE WILD

Albariño is the wine you reach for during the summer when you just can't be bothered. You don't want to overthink what wine to drink, but you don't want anything that would add to the monotony of the day you're having. It's comforting in that it's a dry, crisp white, but the added layer of salinity brings an edge—capable of turning your whole, hot, lethargic day around. So much so, that you find yourself feeling... invigorated. Maybe you *will* go to Whole Foods and buy a filet of cod to grill tonight. You might even put on an actual outfit for dinner, too, instead of cruising through until bedtime in your sweaty athleisure.

A glass of this Albariño inspired you, woke you out of your sleepwalk, and set itself up alongside a beautifully briny piece of grilled fish. What once was a day of languid monotony has ended with an ethereal Galician sunset. If you close your eyes, you're there. So close you can almost smell the salty sea breeze filtering through your landlocked apartment window. Almost.

ASSYRTIKO

THE MOST ICONIC GREEK WINE grape hails from the luxuriously blue Aegean Islands. Originating in Santorini, Assyrtiko has been the staple white wine grape for centuries. And by centuries, I mean since the times of ancient Greece, Caesars and all. But the storied history of this Grecian grape isn't its most interesting quality. The most curious of all is how the Assyrtiko grape has been growing all this time: in contorted, vine-made baskets.

Santorini, and all the Aegean Islands, are as hot as Hades. Situated near the coast of North Africa, the vines are constantly barraged with high-wind heat and intense sun. Sure, Assyrtiko is a hardy grape with deep roots to buffet this environmental vigor. But a vine can only do so much. The solution? Instead of growing Assyrtiko in the standard row-by-row vine setup, exposing the grapes to the fiery elements, winemakers opted for a more *groundbreaking* design.

Assyrtiko grows on vines that sit ground level, coiled around themselves to form a basket. This growing pattern helps protect the grapes from the constant blistering wind and the relentless sun. It's a method not seen anywhere else in the world. No, seriously. Picture it: hundreds of little Assyrtiko vine baskets spaced throughout the dark, volcanic soil of Santorini. To quote Stefano Georgas, winemaker at Estate Argyros, "Santorini is the Jurassic Park of vineyards."

But, like any other national sensation, Assyrtiko has its sights on distant shores. With Santorini well-planted, this vivacious grape has been expanding its reach all over Greece. In Crete, the gentler climate and protective mountains make for a less stressful growing environment. As a result, the wine produced there takes on more fruity and subtly herbaceous flavors, fairly different from the smoky, acidic edge Santorini's soil brings out.

Santorini-grown or not, Assyrtiko is a grape worth becoming acquainted with. Its crisp flavors pack a punch and showcase a terroir that's so uniquely Greek, you can almost taste the volcanic ash.

THE TASTING

THE BOTTLE: *Alexakis Assyrtiko 2019. Crete, Greece. $13.*

Sampling Assyrtiko from Crete instead of Santorini, one can expect a softer, fruit-driven profile. And yet, this bottle of Alexakis brings more Santorini to the table than I expected.

Smelling of passionfruit, lime, and wet concrete, this Cretan variety lives up to its fruit-forward reputation. Although if you smell long enough, and give the glass a few strong swirls while doing so, you might just get a waft of smoke.

The taste is where Assyrtiko shines. The passionfruit kicks off the flavor showdown. Followed up with lemon, spiced vanilla, and a pinch of salt, it's one right after the other. As if that weren't enough to keep you entertained, the alcohol (a strong 13.5%), coupled with a gingery heat, brings up the rear. The heat of this wine spreads like smoke, taking your whole tongue captive. The acidity is high, the alcohol is high, and the heat makes for a wild Aegean rollercoaster of flavor.

Where Albariño holds you with salt, Assyrtiko captivates with a spicy, smoky heat. It's a completely unexpeted sensation in a white wine. Especially one that, on the outside, reads just like a Pinot Grigio—light in every sense of the word. Even when you opt for Crete instead of the original basket grounds of Santorini, the volcanic edge can't help but burst out.

IN THE WILD

Unbeknownst to most passersby, Assyrtiko is a firecracker. Sure, on the outside it's calm, light, and collected, bearing a striking resemblance to the white Pinots. But that's where the similarities end. Assyrtiko only blends in on the outside. Take a sip and you'll rapidly discover just how different it is.

From the jump, you're taken prisoner by the lightning flash of fruit that quickly gives way to spicy ginger heat. The flavors roll over your tongue one after another, creating a spectacle even ancient Greeks would marvel over.

Assyrtiko is anything but tame. From the high alcohol, to the explosion of flavor, to the pops and crackles of acid and spice, you can't help but be entertained. Or at the very least, taken captive. This Grecian grape refuses to back down and insists on wowing every drinker with all the tricks it has. Forget what you thought you knew about white wines from the Mediterranean—Assyrtiko grows to prove that with a little volcanic magic, all flavor bets are off.

CRÉMANT

*To find a French bottle, look in: the Loire, Luxembourg,
Alsace, Burgundy (Crémant de Bourgogne), Jura,
Languedoc-Roussillon (Crémant de Limoux), Bordeaux,
Savoie, and the Rhône (Crémant de Die)*

WHO KNEW THAT FRANCE MADE sparkling wines that aren't Champagne? And who knew there were multiple sparkling wines? Crémant d'Alsace, Crémant de Limoux, Crémant de Bourgogne—the list goes on. All over France, there are nine different regional Crémant wines. This means there are nine distinct non-Champagne sparklers available to us for a much friendlier price tag.

Okay, but what's the catch? Why opt for Crémant over Champagne? Well, the price, for one. Even though both types of sparkling wines undergo a laborious process of secondary fermentation in-bottle, the prices are drastically different. The quality is on par with Champagne, so it's not a lesser caliber of wine that warrants the lower price tag. The aging and grape requirements, however, might have something to do with it. Where Champagne has to age on the lees (dead yeast cells, responsible for the toasty flavors) for at least 12 months, Crémant only has to age for nine. And where Champagne has strict grape requirements, Crémant can be made from any of the well-grown grapes within the region it's produced.

While the longer aging of Champagne produces more mature, full-bodied, complex wines, don't assume Crémant is a far-off second. Champagne is limited in its flavor demonstration, because it's limited in which grapes can be used. Crémant blows the flavor options out of the water. Sure, its aging potential isn't as great, but who can balk at the expansion of varieties at their disposal? In Limoux, the Crémant exudes citrus and apple flavors and is bursting with bright acidity. In the Loire Valley, you'll find a more chalky and mineral edge to its sparklers. And in Burgundy? Expect a richer profile (even more than Champagne!) with bountiful ripe fruit leading the way.

So if you're ever in the mood to spend less money on a less age-worthy (but still high quality) French sparkler, peruse the countryside for a Crémant that speaks your flavor language. You just might find a new favorite French bubbly.

THE TASTING

THE BOTTLE: *Gérard Bertrand Crémant de Limoux Brut Cuvée Thomas Jefferson 2016. Languedoc-Roussillon, France. $15.*

I opted for a Crémant de Limoux as my starting point. Having never tried a Crémant from any region, I had nothing to guide my decision other than the grapes used. I love Chardonnay, Chenin Blanc, and Pinot Noir (the grapes used in this Gérard Bertrand), so I figured I'd be in for a treat.

The color of pale straw and showing a mild display of bubbles, this Crémant appears to be a carbon copy of Champagne. But the aromas... the aromas aren't as similar. Fresh hay, lemon, green apple skin, and the faintest hint of honey prove that Crémant plays its own flavor game. Once you have a taste, it becomes clear how different the two French bubblies can be.

Crémant de Limoux is a mouthful of lemon bar (without powdered sugar), honeycrisp apple skin, and sourdough toast. The reputation of Limoux for being more apple-flavored and full of bright acidity couldn't ring truer. The bubbles explode like Pop Rocks in your mouth. Far more bubbly than I expected, and significantly more aggressive than any Champagne I've tried. But with time, the Crémant calms down. The star-bright acidity and vibrantly crisp apple and citrus flavors tame the more it interacts with oxygen. Interestingly, the more time you give it, the more it presents itself like Champagne. But that's never a problem, is it? Crémant de Limoux sets itself apart, but that doesn't mean it can't win over traditional Champagne lovers either.

IN THE WILD

Crémant is the attention-seeking sister of Champagne. She doesn't get all the attention, respect, and esteem that her sister does. So Crémant incessantly declares that she can do it too! She can be bright, bubbly, and refined—just give her a chance. But when it boils down to it, she'll never be regarded in the same vein. She's not nearly as refined. She's not as age-worthy. Instead, she's "Champagne with an edge." A younger, fruit-driven version of the notorious bubbly. And that's the angle Crémant de Limoux leads with.

Crémant de Limoux is bright, citric, and aggressive. She doesn't try to be buttoned up, doesn't try to fit into the traditional flavor mold. She knows she's different from the grapes alone. She's wild, raw, and edgy. But deep down, she's just as French as her sister. Even though she'll never be Champagne—and doesn't intend to be—if you give her some time, the differences that keep the two apart eventually blur. Or maybe you just start buying into her raw edginess, convinced that Crémant's way is worth a second look. After all, if France is known for anything, it's exceptional sparklers. And they make Crémant *nine* ways to Sunday.

GEWÜRZTRAMINER

To find a French bottle, look in: Alsace

I DON'T KNOW HOW GEWÜRZTRAMINER manages to be overlooked, revered, and wildly polarizing all at the same time, but it does. It's a grape that demands a good unpacking. Naturally, people overlook it, based on its exotic-seeming name and the resultant confusion about how to pronounce it (guh-VURZ-tra-meen-er, in case you were wondering). At least, that was my excuse for the longest time. Can't pronounce it, won't drink it. But since we've cleared that up, we're all one less excuse away from venturing into the white wine world of exotic aromatics.

What sticks out the most about Gewürztraminer is its flavor profile. Unanimously dubbed an "aromatic" wine, its flavors are impossible to ignore. And while aromatic white wines don't have the *best* reputation (looking at you, Moscato), they're not all reminiscent of Bath and Body Works™ body sprays. Still, the framework of this wine's flavor can be polarizing. Much like the vegetal notes of Sauvignon Blanc, Gewürztraminer's sweetly floral notes either impress or offend. Despite winemakers' best efforts to balance out the aromatics with acid, residual sugar, and alcohol, sometimes the florals are just too much for a person's palate.

But regardless of where you land in your flavor preferences, Gewürztraminer is still a noble grape. In Alsace, it's one of the four Grand Cru grapes that have been growing exceptionally for centuries. Since Gewürztraminer doesn't travel well and insists on growing in cool climates, it's limited to where it originated: along the eastern border of France and Germany. Here, in Alsace, it thrives, making it nearly impossible to encounter a sub-par bottle. Whether you end up enjoying its in-your-face flavors or not, Gewürztraminer is an aromatic experience worth trying (at least once).

THE TASTING

THE BOTTLE: *Trimbach Gewürztraminer 2016. Alsace, France. $24.*

Trimbach has been in the Gewürztraminer game since the 1600s. Shocking, right? Over 400 years, and I'm just now getting around to trying it. Better late than never, I suppose. And with a producer that's been around that long, one would assume they know what they're doing. So let's dive in.

For those that are unfamiliar with the lychee fruit, it smells like a rose dipped in fruit cocktail syrup. Open a bottle of Gewürztraminer and you'll see what I mean—lychee is almost always present in any bottle you come across. And Trimbach has it, along with aromas of ripe pear, grapefruit, and the tiniest hint of pine.

In taste, this bottle is a little more dynamic, living up to the sweetly floral and fruity flavors that Gewürztraminer is known for. There's grapefruit, baked yellow apple, lychee, crystalized ginger, and mandarin orange, all dancing on your palate in no particular order. With each successive sip, the order of the flavors shifts. Sometimes lychee appears first, sometimes it's grapefruit, and sometimes the crystallized ginger kicks off while the mandarin finishes. It's always moving with each sip. Much like entering a traffic roundabout, you never know which flavor will follow.

Despite the chaos of flavors, this bottle is highly aromatic and well-balanced. The acidity isn't high, but if you're hit with the grapefruit, it'll feel like it. The same goes for the sweetness. It's not a sweet wine, but with the sweet fruit flavors and medium body, the illusion will get you.

The Trimbach is a genuine display of what a Gewürztraminer can offer: a wild mix of flavors, a sweetly floral impression, and a wine that is anything but subtle.

IN THE WILD

Alsatian Gewürztraminer is an early 2000s pop star. Dressed in neon brights, metallics, and accessories to the nines, it's *a lot* to take in. There's so much going on that flamboyant seems like an understatement. Yet, despite all the seemingly artificial elements, you have to admit you're kind of loving it. Even though its songs use elements of other popular tunes, their unique twist on it is nothing short of a bop. A guilty pleasure if there ever was one.

Gewürztraminer is just that. It's loud, in-your-face, and its combination of flavors is seen nowhere else. The notes seem to dance around chaotically, making no sense on paper. Yet for some, it all magically works. A top-notch glass of Gewürztraminer is exaggerated, shimmying, and keeps you coming back for more. Plus, like any good pop song from the early 2000s, it's ironically timeless. Keep it on deck for a while; it'll only get better.

GRÜNER VELTLINER

YOU CAN'T START DABBLING WITH Austrian wines until you go through their gatekeeper: the infamous Grüner Veltliner. It would be like sampling from Australia and not trying Shiraz. Or hopping over to Germany and not tasting Riesling. These wines are their nations' pride and joy. And although Shiraz and Riesling can be made well elsewhere, Austria has an exclusive on great Grüner.

In Central Europe, each country has its own wine star. One wine to cultivate, exact, and disperse as the high-quality representative of their nation. In Germany, it's the aromatic and highly acidic Riesling. In Hungary, it's the dual-nature Furmint that shines as both a sweet and a bone-dry wine. With Austria, it's no different. Grüner Veltliner has become their high-quality stunner, slowly but surely penetrating wine markets around the world.

From one friend to another, I know that it's difficult to care about *yet another light, crisp, white wine.* There are already too many to distract and confuse you when you're trying to select a bottle for the weekend. Why bother with a lesser-known country and a weirdly named varietal when you can kick back with another bottle of Sauvignon Blanc?

For one, Austria consistently makes Grüner Veltliner well. It's not growing in suspect plots all over the world where it can't thrive. It's grown almost exclusively (94%) in a country that treasures it. So it's virtually impossible to get your hands on a bad bottle. But if that's not convincing enough, there's one particular wine audience that might be interested. For all the Sauvignon Blanc lovers out there, Grüner's coming for you.

THE TASTING

THE BOTTLE: *Markus Huber Vision Grüner Veltliner 2019. Traisental, Austria. $14.*

Yeah, I said it. Grüner is a worthy replacement for Sauvignon Blanc. One taste, and you'll understand why.

Truth be told, I'm a little biased against Sauv Blanc. I declared in the first book of this wine-loving series that the mown-grass flavors of SB and I do not get along. But my opinion aside, Grüner Veltliner has merits that stand on its own.

The Huber Vision starts out strong, with aromas of lemon, nectarine, and Anjou pear. A classic, crisp, white wine. Adding a pinch of lime and a surprising dash of white pepper sets the flavors of Grüner apart from the rest. The zesty combo of fruit and citrus makes the whole flavor profile lively. And it tastes like it was all poured over flat, rounded pond pebbles, adding a unique layer of minerality. When you finally enter the white pepper finish, prepare to enjoy its savory, diffused heat that's strikingly different from the piquant bite of black pepper.

Where it can sharply veer into Sauvignon Blanc territory is on the first few sips. Pay close enough attention, and you might just get hints of cold edamame (tossed in white pepper, naturally). Still believe you don't have room in your wine arsenal for yet another light, crisp white? Think again.

IN THE WILD

Grüner Veltliner is the young hotshot, looking to take the reins from Sauvignon Blanc. It's livelier, spicier, and much less grassy than its classic counterpart. It's the type that would slide you its business card when you're already doing business with Sauv Blanc—sure, you might not want to stray, since Sauv has been with you since your early 20s. But the confidence and charisma that Grüner brings are enough to make you reconsider. Especially if you're tired of the same old grassy song and dance that Sauvignon offers every time you sit down with it. Who knows? You might find a new crisp, palate-cleansing, subtly green, white wine that'll sweep you off your feet, if only to remind you that Sauvignon Blanc isn't the only herby heartthrob at your disposal.

MELON DE BOURGOGNE

To find a French bottle, look in: the Loire (Muscadet)

IF ALBARINO IS THE CRISP, seafood-friendly white of Spain, then Melon de Bourgogne is its French counterpart. Confusingly grown in the Loire Valley, not in Burgundy, as you might think from the name, the 'Bourgogne' identifier is nothing more than a historical reference. Once upon a time, in 1709, the Loire Valley experienced a nasty frost that destroyed many a grape. To bring the Loire back to life, Burgundian monks helpfully transplanted a frost-hearty grape from Burgundy—the Melon de Bourgogne. Ever since, it's been a Loire citizen. And thriving, I might add.

Since its relocation, Melon has kept growing and improving in quality. The increase in the quality of its wines is not only attributed to the heartiness of the grape, but to the surge of individual growers. This surge is attributed to the fact that Melon was outright banned from Burgundy in the 18th century in favor of the Chardonnay grape. Rude, right? But boxing it out from Burgundy gave the winemakers in the Loire even more reason to hunker down with this delicious, vineyard-saving grape. Since then, Melon has been the white grape of choice in the Loire, thanks to its enduring nature and resistance to frost.

Now, centuries later, the rest of the world is getting excited about Melon, too. How can you not be? When turned into Muscadet wine, it's a crisp, minerally, and zippier version of Chablis (without the price tag). Plus, Muscadet doesn't just delight when it's lean, fresh, and young. When it's aged sur lie (in the bottle with its natural yeasts), the depth of toasty flavor brings the wine to a whole new level. And it's priced to sell (and drink!), making it an affordable treat and a friendly option for the anti-fruity-white-wine crowd.

Call it by its grape (Melon de Bourgogne) or call it by its wine (Muscadet), but this little Loire number is just getting started.

THE TASTING

THE BOTTLE: *Domaine de la Pépière La Pépie Sur Lie (Muscadet Sèvre et Main) 2018. Muscadet, France. $15.*

One of the major producers of Muscadet, Domaine de la Pépière regularly churns out quality wines at affordable price points. With notes of lemon, herbs, and bread dough on the nose, it's easy to see how Sauvignon Blanc and Champagne lovers take a liking to the aromas of Muscadet.

The flavors aren't a far cry from the nose: lemon, green apple skin, green pear, wet rocks, and bread all come together in one crisp, bone-dry package. The acidity is so prevalent that I would call this bottle of Muscadet the wine equivalent of lemon zest. It's citrusy, a little herbal, and topped off with polarizing wet gravel notes and a hint of bread. As punchy as it is, it's shockingly well-balanced.

When choosing between dry white wines, avid wine drinkers should consider Muscadet as part of their rotation. The acidity is there. The dryness is there. And the curious balance of herbs, minerals, and bread is enough to make it interesting. Pair it beautifully with seafood or enjoy it as a summer apéritif. Either way, Muscadet will shine right through.

IN THE WILD

In terms of flavor and personality (not the DNA of the grape), Muscadet is the sophisticated older sister of Pinot Grigio and the cousin to Sauvignon Blanc—she carries the best of both and the worst of neither. She's the favorite of the family because she always impresses, never causes trouble, and still is far from a wet blanket or wallflower. She's happy waiting for her chance to shine, because she knows that when that time comes, she'll blow everyone away with her presence. She's direct, refined, and yet still has something about her you can't stay away from.

Bring her around anyone; she'll wow the company by simply being herself. Which, of course, will make you want to bring her around more often. Before you know it, you'll be wondering what took you so long to acquaint yourself with the lovely French Loire stunner—and how you ever lived without her.

PINOT BLANC

To find a French bottle, look in: Alsace

WHEN YOU SAY "PINOT", TWO grapes immediately come to mind: Noir and Gris. The former being a world-renowned red known for its superb quality and ability to delight almost any palate, and the latter being a mutation of the Noir, producing the most reached-for "neutral" white, full of crisp fruit and acidity. Pinot Gris is known to please just about any white wine drinker. If Pinot Noir is the red grape in the herd, and Pinot Gris is the curiously grey one ("gris" means grey in French), then all we're missing from the color wheel is a true white variety. Cue Pinot Blanc, the final grape to round out the Pinot spectrum of color.

Like its relative Pinot Gris, Pinot Blanc is also a mutation of the Pinot Noir grape. While Pinot Noir has the most anthocyanin (a component responsible for its purple color), Pinot Blanc has the least. Pinot Gris is the stubborn middle child between the two, splitting the difference in anthocyanin. But how does that genetic, scientific fact affect flavor?

As you may know from the first leg of this wine journey, Pinot Gris/Grigio is its own testament to regional differences in winemaking and terroir. You can get an Alsatian Pinot Gris that's wildly different from its Italian Grigio counterpart. But Pinot Blanc has some versatility up its sleeve, too.

On its own, Pinot Blanc is usually less acidic than Pinot Gris and carries more fruit, spice, and occasional smoke flavors. With its more mellow structure, Pinot Blanc is often used as a blending grape, too, even becoming sparkling or sweet wines. When blended with Chardonnay, the highly successful Italian Pinot Bianco wine is born. In Italy, they also showcase Pinot Blanc as the main grape in their lesser-known sparkling wine, Franciacorta. Head over to France and *their* lesser-known sparkling wine, Crémant, can be made with Pinot Blanc, when it's referred to as Crémant d'Alsace. The options are endless for this versatile Pinot mutation.

Whether grown in France, Italy, Germany, Hungary, or Austria, the Pinot Blanc grape will find a way to contribute either on its own or blended with your favorites. As a still, sparkling, or sweet wine, this lesser-known Pinot fills the gaps where Noir and Gris can't.

THE TASTING

THE BOTTLE: *Kracher Pinot Blanc Trocken 2017. Burgenland, Austria. $18.*

I opted for a Pinot Blanc from Austria to broaden my wine horizons. As an Austrian wine novice, I know little about their wine-producing style apart from Grüner Veltliner. But I *do* know that "trocken" means dry, so I shouldn't be expecting a saccharine kiss on the mouth.

With aromas of stone fruit, ripe pineapple, and citrus, I now realize that the smoke and spice flavors common to Pinot Blanc must be unique to the varieties from Alsace (the smoky white wine capital of the world). Just another reason to sample grape varieties from all over the world, I guess.

In taste, Austria's Pinot Blanc differs greatly from what I had expected. With under-ripe peach, gravel, and lemon zest flavors, I'm surprised at the level of acidity present. Normally deemed the less acidic version of Pinot Gris, this bottle of Blanc is edging itself closer to Gris than I would have anticipated. Regardless, it's not out of place. It's so light that you'd almost forget you just sipped if it weren't for the lingering acid.

If Melon de Bourgogne and Pinot Gris had a baby, it would be Austrian Pinot Blanc. The stone fruit flavor is there, but it isn't the dominant trait. The acidity and minerality are the dominant ones, with the gravel flavor hitting early. Overall, like most light whites, it's crisp and decently acidic—an easy swap for Pinot Grigio or even an unoaked Chardonnay.

IN THE WILD

The Austrian Pinot Blanc is no-fuss and uncomplicated. It's straight and to the point, delivering exactly what you need from it—stone fruit, a light, watery body, and a splash of acidity. It's not too much of anything, making it the most affable white wine on the shelf. You can enjoy it six ways to Sunday, whether with food, on its own, as a palate cleanser, or a last-minute aperitif. Ice cold, room temperature, or lightly chilled. No matter how you enjoy it, Pinot Blanc will deliver; it's reliable that way. You don't have to stress about it. A true set-it-and-forget-it kind of white wine. And the best part is, you can watch it showcase its versatility each time you sample it from a new country. Much like its sibling Pinot Noir, Pinot Blanc is for anyone and everyone. Point *Blanc*.

ROUSSANNE

*To find a French bottle, look in: the northern Rhône (St.
Joseph, Hermitage, Crozes-Hermitage), and southern
Rhône (Côtes du Rhône)*

ROUSSANNE IS A BIT OF an enigma. Not because its flavors
are hard to figure out, or because it's unpredictable, like Pinot
Noir. The true mystery is that it's not a common monovarietal—
you rarely encounter a wine made solely from Roussanne. It's
always Roussanne "and." Roussanne and Marsanne.
Roussanne and Viognier. Roussanne and five others. Ask any
French oenophile and they'll gladly fawn over how aromatic,
acidic, and elegant the grape is. Yet you'd be hard-pressed to
find it outside of a blend. Why would such a seemingly lovely
white wine grape never get the opportunity to stand alone?

The answer undoubtedly lies with the ones who cultivate it. The French grow their grapes with intent. And in my humble opinion, they intend to always knock it out of the park, to cultivate an immaculate harvest. The French produce the most sophisticated, austere, powerful, and surreal wines in the world. And every wine falls into one of two categories: stunning monovarietal or star-studded ensemble. In the northern Rhône, the reds are made from Syrah and Syrah alone. In Sancerre, there's only Sauvignon Blanc. On the flip side, Bordeaux magically blends Cabernet Sauvignon, Merlot, and Cabernet Franc. A collaboration that, when made only in France, warrants price tags that mere mortals would balk at.

So then what's the deal with Roussanne? If it's so lovely and wonderful, why isn't it being touted as a stunning monovarietal? Because, believe it or not, even when French wine growers cultivate a beautiful grape like Roussanne, sometimes it still needs more to shine. Usually a little… je ne sais quoi. A concept inherently French and completely outside of my American understanding.

Much like Cabernet Franc, Roussanne *can* be grown on its own, but when blended with others, it seems to reach new heights. We all know that peanut butter sandwiches are good, but peanut butter and jelly? Infinitely better. The same goes for Roussanne. Marsanne is the jelly to Roussanne's peanut butter. Whether you want a peanut butter sandwich or a PB&J is entirely up to you and your taste buds. But if I've learned anything, it's that the French don't make wine mistakes. If they intend for a grape to blend, it's usually for good reasons.

THE TASTING

THE BOTTLE: *Yves Cuilleron Roussanne Les Vignes d'a Cote 2018. Rhône Valley, France. $23.*

I've never been one to want just a peanut butter sandwich. Put jelly on it, or don't even bother. But we're dealing with wine here. And that means you have to try everything once. It would be unfair of me to assume Roussanne by itself couldn't placate before I gave it a fair chance. So, Yves Cuilleron, you're up.

The aromatics live up to Roussanne's reputation: apricot, white flowers, peach, plastic wax, and wet rocks. A grab bag of florals, stone fruit, and hints of minerality. It's right on par with a classic Viognier. But that's where the similarities end, and where the need for a blending partner begins.

The flavors are fleeting. At first, you get hit with peach and beeswax flavors, followed shortly thereafter by white tea, wet rocks, and finally, baking spices. The varying flavors aren't surprising; what's surprising is how none of them last in your mouth. It's fairly flat in delivery, not suspended by dominant fruit, citrus, or any other flavors that hold the taste up.

In all fairness, this bottle offers what one should expect from Roussanne in any capacity. It's acidic, light, and refreshing. And if you continue, it starts to vaguely resemble a California Chardonnay, albeit with much less depth and body. Overall, the flavor sensation leaves much to be desired. It's like catching a Roussanne-flavored bubble in your mouth—the flavor is only on the surface, with nothing on the inside.

I now see the reason this grape rarely gets the solo star treatment. So it goes with Roussanne, I guess. For some, this Yves Cuilleron peanut butter sandwich suffices. For me, I need the jelly.

IN THE WILD

French Roussanne is the yin to Marsanne's yang, part of the sister act, not a soloist. Roussanne is shy, withdrawn, and not trying to hog the spotlight. Her flavors are there, but not for long. She knows that on her own, she'll only scratch the surface of the greatness that's available when she performs alongside her sister. She practically begs for her rich, textured counterpart to come along and save her. Together, they're unstoppable. Together, they're a dream team. But on her own, Roussanne would rather smile and nod politely via fleeting fruit flavors and a quick finish of spices. Her enduring minerality and mild, waxy tea flavors remain steadfast in the interim. Roussanne isn't a bore or a burden. She's not sullen and lifeless. But one can't ignore the fact that she was made to shine in tandem with her

Rhône partner, Marsanne. Only then does she truly sparkle and come to life. Just the way the French intended it.

SEMILLON

*To find a French bottle, look in: Bordeaux (Graves,
Pessac-Léognan, Sauternes, Barsac)*

IN TERMS OF UNDERRATED WINES, Semillon is top of
the list. For those wine drinkers who stick to what they know
(hello, most of us), crossing paths with a bottle of Semillon is
unlikely. Which isn't surprising, considering it's like a crocodile
in the wine world, barely noticeable to surface-level onlookers,
but those submerged in the depths can't miss it. If you happen
to be floating on a riverboat, let me catch you up to speed on
what's lurking below.

Semillon is a wine of threes. It's grown superbly in three
countries: France (Bordeaux, primarily), Australia (Western,
Southern, and Hunter Valley), and South Africa, to a lesser

extent. It also presents itself in three wildly different ways: a lusciously sweet variety (in Sauternes and Barsac, for example), a rich and silky oaked variety, and finally, a light and crisp variety. Good luck not finding a bottle you like—Semillon covers the spectrum of wine drinkers.

But no matter where you sample from or what style you prefer, Semillon has the unique ability to age well. Unlike red wines, most white wines aren't known for getting better with time. They're rarely produced with cellaring potential and, as a result, are normally drunk young. Not Semillon. Sure, its manifestation as a sweet dessert wine (the most famous being the French Sauternes) is expected to keep for years. And yeah, maybe a rich oaky white variety could handle extra aging. But you just don't find a dry, crisp, white wine that can age beyond two years. That's what makes Semillon so dynamic. Some of the best dry varieties can be cellared for *15 years*.

It doesn't matter if you buy it from France or Australia. Whether it's dry, sweet, or oaked, anyone can enjoy Semillon. Either now, six months from now, or in a decade, Semillon will always be ready for you.

THE TASTING

THE BOTTLE: *Brokenwood Hunter Valley Semillon 2018. Hunter Valley, Australia. $19.*

For my tasting, I've opted for the popular dry variety from Hunter Valley. Here, the climate is cooler, so it's safe to expect a lot of citrus and crispness from their white varieties. Hunter Valley Semillons also have a reputation for being able to develop upon aging. As these wines age, they can easily transform into a more toasty, nutty version of themselves. Fascinating.

But this is a 2018, being enjoyed in 2020, so I expect the crispness to still be very much intact. And that's precisely what I got. Aromas of chalk, lemon rind, lime, and wet stones are the introduction. The flavors of rainwater, green apple, beeswax, and lemon-lime club soda settle in abruptly on the first sip. I've got to say, I've never had a wine taste as... *fresh* as this bottle of Semillon. It tastes like drinking a glass of rainwater that had natural green apple flavoring added to it. With a slightly chalky delivery, too.

Give it time, and the rainwater essence steps aside to allow room for the lemon-lime club soda and beeswax to come forth. The acidity is laser-focused, settling in on the front center of your tongue, a speed bump for the flavors to linger for a moment before dissipating. A water-like (in body and flavor) white wine, this Semillon brings freshness to a whole new level.

IN THE WILD

Hunter Valley Semillon is a dry, peace-loving, Zen-like, free spirit, always encouraging you to keep calm, meditate, and focus on the positives. Sure, it's bright and colorful, but the modus operandi is being one with nature. Natural is best with Semillon, and they'll all but shove that natural freshness down your throat. Even if you choke on its organic qualities at first. But spend a little time with it, and its quirks start to become soothing. You realize that you'll only get these Zen characteristics for a short period, so you might as well buckle down in lotus pose and relax. After all, in a few years, Semillon will be a completely different character.

SOAVE

EVERY TIME I READ OR hear the name 'Soave', I immediately sing it to the tune of Volare by Dean Martin. "Soooooo-ahhh-vey, ohhhh, ohh." And now you'll start doing it, too. But you can't help it with Italian wines. They set themselves up in a fantastic little niche all their own. It's not my fault that Soave is an upbeat, casual, kind of Italian wine— perfect for rhyming with Volare. In fact, I call that Italian kismet.

Singing aside, what does this little white Italian musical number bring to the table? Comfort, style, and approachability. Made from the Garganega grape, Soave has been produced since medieval times. If you ever get the chance to go to its namesake town in Italy, you'll even see a castle in the center. So you know the Italians hold this one near and dear.

Known for its dry, fruity, and crisp, light-bodied style, Soave is right up there with Pinot Grigio as one of Italy's top whites. Unfortunately, many producers shoot for quantity over quality, so finding a merely pedestrian bottle is commonplace. But there is a way to avoid this pitfall: opt for a Soave Classico. Bottles with this designation are made in the traditional winemaking region of Veneto, representing the higher quality of winemaking and terroir that this wine is praised for.

In true Italian fashion, there's even a sparkling option for this lovely wine, too. Opt for a Soave Spumante and delight in its fun, fruity, and even vanilla-like flavors. Whether spumante or still, Soave can sit alongside almost any occasion, food, or Dean Martin song. *Sooooo-ahhh-vey.*

THE TASTING

THE BOTTLE: *Inama Soave Classico 2019. Veneto, Italy. $15.*

Inama is known as a consistently high-quality producer, and at $15, trying them out is a bet with few downsides. With lemon, gravel, gardenia, and white peach aromas, this Soave Classico stays true to its dry, crisp reputation. Not terribly fruit-forward, the peach and lemon flavors come through subtly. But the wet gravel minerality is the most dominant flavor at play. This bottle tastes like drinking water that had gummy lemon candy and gravel soaking in it. If you're a fan of minerally whites, this bottle is right up your alley.

The Inama is simple—nothing complicated in terms of flavor or body. It's light-bodied, mildly acidic, and subdued in its flavor profile. Compared to a Pinot Gris, it feels lighter, based on its simplicity. But it's neck-and-neck with the Italian Grigio style, naturally. Swap in a Soave Classico for the Pinot Grigio anytime you have an unpredictable menu at hand or are just getting the evening started. It'll settle in nicely wherever you lead it.

IN THE WILD

Soave is a gateway wine. The wine you slap on the table before you even decide what food you're getting, let alone look at a menu. It doesn't matter what food you order—or if you even order any. There are no requirements with Soave. It's delicate, mild, and palate-cleansing. You don't have to overthink it, it's basic—the white tee of white wine. Italian whites are reliable that way. Where Pinot Gris is more elegant, Soave is elevated casual. Dare I say, Soave would even be down for a sweatpants kind of night. Who knows? Maybe this lovely gateway white will usher you into real pants after a glass or two. But that's between you and Soave. Just know that it'll go wherever you do, and it'll soothe you with every drop along the way.

TORRONTÉS

TORRONTES IS AN ARGENTINIAN BLAST-IN-A-GLASS.
At least the Riojano variety, of which I'm solely familiar, is.
Technically, Torrontés isn't just one type of white wine; it's
three. Even though all three Torrontés wines are nearly identical
in terms of the grapes involved, the flavors and aromas are
distinct. Torrontés Riojano is the more aromatic and high-
quality variety of the three (and the most widely planted).
Torrontés Sanjuanino is a step down from Riojano in both flavor
expression and overall quality. Typically, Sanjuanino is
reserved for table wine. Finally, there's the Torrontés
Mendocino—known as the black sheep of the three, its

plantings are steadily declining, and its flavors and aromas aren't on par with the other two.

But let's not cry over spilled wine. Torrontés is a truly special variety that, if produced anywhere else, would never live up to its potential. Its grapes thrive in the aggressive, dry heat and high-altitude of vineyards along the edges of the Andes. Thriving in this climate is a feat few white grapes could handle. Yet, despite the rigorous growing environment, Torrontés is bursting with life.

It's aromatic like a Riesling, dry and pungent like a Sauvignon Blanc, and sometimes salty and acidic like an Albariño. Where Vinho Verde fails at combining popular white wine grapes' traits, Torrontés excels. It took all the best flavors of the others and cranked up the saturation to a whole new level. And it works in every way. There's a reason Argentina has pumped up the production for this wine over the years—the world just can't get enough.

THE TASTING

THE BOTTLE: *Susana Balbo Crios Torrontés 2018. Mendoza, Argentina. $12.*

For those of you who read my previous book, *From Cabernet to Zinfandel*, you might remember Susana Balbo. She is a star producer of the Argentinian Malbec. Naturally, I had to go back to her to see how she worked with Argentina's second most-loved grape. Plus, spending $12 on a bottle of Torrontés from *any* Argentinian producer will almost always bring you an enjoyable tasting experience. A steal if I ever saw one.

Susana's Crios Torrontés smells like a New Zealand Sauv Blanc doppelganger: peach, leafy herbs, lemon, and white flowers. In the glass, its color borders between pale straw and light green. If I were in a blind tasting, I'd be suckered into slapping an N.Z. S.B. on it and calling it a day. But the white flower aromas keep it distinct.

Once you sip, you're introduced to ripe passionfruit, pear, sage, lemon, and salt. After loving on some Albariño, I will now dive headfirst into any wine that makes me feel like I'm drinking a little of the ocean along with it. But the overall "1-2 punch" of successive flavors in this bottle of Torrontés is what's impressive. You get socked in the mouth with ripe passionfruit and pear flavors cut with lemon, only to be treated to a follow-up knockout of salt and soaring acid.

Don't be fooled by the fruits; this wine is dry. But it's hard to tell at first, considering your mouth seeps with passionfruit and pear from the minute your tongue hits the wine. Luckily, the fruit flavors aren't the only dominating forces at play. The classic New Zealand Sauvignon Blanc leafy flavors contribute, too. Oh, and don't forget about the lemony acid and salty flavors that Albariño is so famous for. These powerful flavor elements combine to make an insane flavor experience unlike any I've had with white wine (see what I mean about wines changing your expectations?). The big rush of fruits and green flavors followed by the acid and salt is like a steep drop in a rollercoaster—you either love the sensation or immediately regret it. Welcome to Torrontés, everybody.

IN THE WILD

Argentinian Torrontés is the hibachi grill of the white wine world. Sure, on the outside, it looks like any other restaurant. But inside, spotting that imposing flattop grill, you know that you're in for an unexpected thrill. The notes of sage and leafy herbs, bearing an uncanny resemblance to a New Zealand Sauvignon Blanc, let you know the same. You're open to new experiences, though. That's why you opted for the "hibachi Torrontés"—you wanted something new, something unexpected. And that's precisely what you get.

As soon as that fire ignites, you're both dazzled and vexed. You're captivated by the grandiose display, but wondering how it doesn't burn the entire place down, rendering the entire experience a nightmare. The Torrontés comes to life in much the same way. The bursting forth of ripe fruit flavors coupled with the green notes that make Sauvignon Blanc so polarizing. The flame of flavors growing higher with the addition of salt and acid. How can it all coexist and not fall apart? And how on earth did you go so long without experiencing it for yourself?

Maybe the next time you're out, you'll turn towards Torrontés. You know it'll be nothing short of a rip-roaring good time.

VERDEJO

SURPRISE, SURPRISE. WHAT DO WE have here? Another underappreciated white wine? You betcha—Spanish Verdejo is the definition of "low-key" in the wine world. In fact, it wasn't until the 1980s that anyone, Spanish or not, started paying any attention to it. Shoutout to Marques de Riscal, a Riojan producer, for "discovering" and bringing it into the limelight of top Spanish white wines.

And yet here I am, decades later, still with no clue what this wine is all about. Even despite its rescue from obscurity in the 80s, Verdejo is a wine that few will come across. It's not incredibly popular as a dry, aromatic white wine—a competitive ranking in which many will try, few will conquer. Plus, Verdejo only grows in Rueda, Spain. The poor-quality soil there ironically brings out the best in this overlooked grape. So, it's not like it's popping up in vineyards all over the world. And, to add insult to injury, nobody ever goes to Rueda on their visit to Spain!

But the good news is that being privy to Verdejo automatically makes you a wine insider. It's hard to come across, but you'll have unlocked a new white wine to fawn over. And for those who love Sauvignon Blanc, Torrontés, or even a fruity Pinot Gris, you'll love what Verdejo offers. It's bright, aromatic, and bursting with fruity and herbaceous flavors. At the risk of ushering this poor little wine into obscurity *again,* I vote we all give little "V" its due.

THE TASTING

THE BOTTLE: *Protos Verdejo 2018. Rueda, Spain. $11.*

For $11, I'll gladly experiment with an overlooked white wine. Even if it comes as a recommended alternative to Sauvignon Blanc. We all know how I feel about Sauv Blanc (it's a no from me, dog), so I'm going in hoping for fewer herbs, more fruit.

Protos delivers. On the nose, there's green apple, lime pith, passionfruit, almond, and leafy green herbs (sage, eucalyptus). A lot going on in the sensory department already. But the first sip is nothing compared to the smell. It damn near knocked me backward.

Lime, green apple skin, blanched almonds (in other words, almonds without their skins), and wet slate all swirl together in a highly acidic vortex. But if you give it a minute or two, the mellow almond and wet slate flavors temper out the vibrant fruit and citrus. At least until the finish. There's a fun little kick of ginger heat at the end—you know, just in case the slap in the mouth of lime and acid wasn't enough.

The flavors are explosive, bright, and ripe as day. It feels like there's a tiny wine wizard in my mouth squeezing out alternating rain clouds of lime- and lemon-flavored precipitation. For the Sauv Blanc lovers, you'll be happy to know that this bottle of Protos does indeed have an herbal bite to it—it's just less green bell pepper, more leafy herb.

Verdejo lives up to its reputation as a white wine Spanish flamenco. The varying flavors all dance in rotation, making every effort to keep you on your toes while still staying true to the light white wine choreography. ¡Olé! all day.

IN THE WILD

Verdejo is that one person who always makes sure everyone has a good time but, for whatever reason, always does a little too much. On vacation, they cram in as many exotic, entertaining excursions as possible, thinking the group might fall asleep otherwise. When choosing a restaurant, they go for anything with a "wow" factor. God forbid there's flaming cheese on the menu; that's their restaurant kryptonite. And forget throwing a low-key party with Verdejo. No, no; they're going all out with a theme from head to toe. Even if that means letting Pinterest explode all over their kitchen with hyper-thematic decor and intricate setups. But that's why we keep them around. Despite their over-the-top efforts, they always make sure you have a good time. And for that, Verdejo, we love you.

VINHO VERDE

VINHO VERDE IS SO TRANSPARENT, it's almost endearing. When you dive into the world of wine, it's hard to understand a lot of varieties and their nuances. Syrah has multiple regional expressions; Chardonnay is in everything, showing up as a unique character each time; Merlot suffers from being made almost too well in Bordeaux and seems to fall short everywhere else. But Vinho Verde? She's as easy to understand as it gets. The only misconception is that Vinho Verde isn't a grape, but a blend from the Vinho Verde region in Portugal.

Outside of its name appropriation, this Portuguese white wine reads like water: light, consistent, and goes with everything. Oh, and sometimes it's carbonated. It's true! Back in the day, Vinho Verde was bottled so quickly that fermentation had to finish in the bottle. This lead to a surprisingly fizzy wine that caught many off-guard. Nowadays, producers will artificially add carbonation to carry on that reputation that the world has grown to enjoy. Although, these days, many smaller wineries are opting to push out still varieties over fizzy ones.

Carbonated or not, Vinho Verde brings out a limited, yet delightful, spectrum of flavor. Citrus, tropical fruit, stone fruit, and light minerality are the name of the game with this white wine. It's always acidic, always full of fruit, and sometimes minerally—never aged in oak or altered in sweetness.

On top of Vinho's consistency of flavor, it can also pair with almost everything outside of red meat. Seafood? Stellar pairing. Sushi? Just as solid. Salads and pasta? Absolutely. A hodgepodge meal of potatoes and pork? Bring it on! Whether you're salivating over seafood, crunching through vegetables and herbs, or slurping up a rich garlic sauce, Vinho Verde can complement it perfectly. A reliable wine through and through (and with an average $10 price tag), Vinho Verde is an easy swap for your favorite light white, no matter the occasion.

THE TASTING

THE BOTTLE: *Casa do Valle Vinho Verde 2019. Douro Valley, Portugal. $9.*

In the debate on fizzy vs. still, Casa do Valle falls on the still side. Not a problem, though, seeing as how the aromas shine through this bottle, clear as day. With wafts of lemon pith, grapefruit, and wet gravel, the aromatic consistency of Vinho Verde brings a smile to my wine-thirsty face. One sip seals it.

There's lemon zest, overripe pineapple, and pear flavors barreling through. The predictability of flavors is almost comforting. You know you won't be surprised with hints of oak, varying sweetness, or high levels of alcohol. It's nearly the same story every time.

The acidity is bright with a long finish, carrying the pineapple and pear flavors with it. The fruits, the citrus, and the acid all play together nicely. Although it's a dry, light wine through and through, this bottle pushes the boundaries. When you taste, it gives off the illusory sensation that it's fuller than, say, a Muscadet, due to the dominance of tropical fruit flavor. And when slightly warmer than chilled, it can even give off an oily texture akin to a South African Chenin Blanc.

If Sauvignon Blanc from New Zealand, Chenin Blanc from South Africa, and Muscadet all had a weird three-parent baby, it'd be this bottle of Vinho Verde. It's dry, tropical, and sparkling with acidity. But it's still casual—nothing fussy or buttoned up about it. And for $9, I can't complain.

IN THE WILD

Vinho Verde is a white wine chameleon trying to blur the lines between itself and the other popular white wines. It's got the prevailing tropical fruit flavor that Sauvignon Blancs from New Zealand are famous for. It has the illusory medium body spurred on by its dominant fruit and oily texture, like Chenin Blanc from South Africa. And, even still, it maintains a sky-high acidity like that of Muscadet.

Vinho Verde is trying to hang out with all the heavy hitters by pointing out their shared qualities. It appeals to a wide variety of white wine lovers and goes with almost any light meal you set next to it. As a result, it doesn't set itself apart as a distinct entity. You could say it suffers from an identity crisis, trying to be like all the others. And while it's certainly a pleasant and palatable white wine, Vinho Verde isn't a unique individual.

Sure, it's consistent and quaffable, and sometimes that's just what you need. And should you find yourself surrounded by white wine lovers who can't seem to agree, Vinho Verde might be the one to pacify everyone. So its imitative qualities aren't always a bad thing. Sometimes consistency, reliability, and affordability are exactly what the sommelier ordered. And if it is, you know Vinho Verde will always be there.

VIOGNIER

To find a French bottle, look in: the northern Rhône (Condrieu, Château-Grillet), the southern Rhône (Côtes-du-Rhône), and Languedoc-Roussillon (varietally named Vin de Pays d'Oc)

ONE CAN'T HELP BUT FEEL slightly more elegant when selecting a chic-sounding wine like Viognier. It screams French class and elegance, and yet it barely escaped extinction back in the 1960s. As a late bloomer and fussy grape, Viognier is no walk in the park for winemakers. It requires plentiful sunshine to fully ripen, but if it gets too hot, its flavors disintegrate. It's susceptible to disease, but if you wanted to replant it elsewhere, you'd need to completely revamp the drainage of your soil. So Viognier can be quite the headache for vintners.

Nevertheless, when you get it right, Viognier is an aromatic beauty unparalleled in its ability to finely balance perfume and fruit. Where Muscat is overwhelming with its perfumed aromatics, Viognier is delicate. Where Chardonnay is dominant in fruit flavors, Viognier is balanced. It straddles the line between aromatic and rich in a way other white wines can't pull off. And thanks to a few venerable wineries in Australia and California during the 1970s, we all still get to enjoy this magnificent grape.

Whether you choose a variety from the Northern Rhône, Southern Australia, or Northern California, Viognier will make you feel as though you stopped to smell the roses. In the least cheesy way possible, of course.

THE TASTING

THE BOTTLE: *Cline North Coast Viognier 2019. Sonoma Valley, CA. $12.*

Feeling confident that I'd find a delightful Viognier no matter where I traveled, I decided on a bottle from Sonoma. Right off the bat, aromas of bosc pear, honeysuckle (a key giveaway that you're sipping an aromatic white), and white roses pour out from the glass. The florals are as clear as day—like you're traipsing through an English rose garden.

The aromas carry through to the taste. The citrus, honey-like flavor of honeysuckle, soft tangerine, subtle apricot, and drops of rosewater permeate every inch of your tongue. The soft fruits perfectly balance the florals, creating a buoy of flavor. It's elegant, soft, and slightly oily in its delivery. And in terms of the body, it's right on par with an oaked Chardonnay. Put a chill on it and the rosy perfume becomes even softer, more delicate.

While this bottle of Cline is technically dry, the impression it gives off is that of a sweeter variety. The dynamics between the tangerine flavor and the honeysuckle lead you to believe that it's sweeter than it is. It's this sweetness sleight of hand that makes Viognier a perfect offering for a mixed crowd of *dry-hard* wine lovers and aromatic aficionados. And with its gorgeous aromatics, you can't help but dedicate Viognier to the most timeless women in your life. Let's be honest, the resemblance is uncanny.

IN THE WILD

Unsurprisingly, Viognier is the wine equivalent of Elizabeth James in the Parent Trap (the 1998 version). And no better scene captures her essence than the one where "Annie" (Hallie) is scanning her mom's bedroom, admiring her chic baubles and vanity trimmings while "Here Comes the Sun" plays in the background. The impression she gathers of her mother in that scene is the exact impression Viognier leaves. Allow me to acquaint you.

Elizabeth's bedroom is painted a perfectly mature dusty pink, with curated white bouquets of flowers intentionally placed throughout. In the background, you hear her on the phone speaking fluently in French as if she were serenading whoever was on the other line. Panning over to the timeless wooden vanity, her jewelry is glimmering amidst pristine black velvet displays, only dared to be traced with a feather-light touch. Everything on the vanity top is either housed in sparkling crystal or immaculately polished silver—the lamp with the crystal chandelier trimmings, the petite charcoal drawing of a woman's face, the handheld mirror fit for a Disney princess. None of which are deemed too gaudy or antiquated. A portrayal that captures as much of Elizabeth James as it does Viognier. Chic, romantic, feminine, and timeless.

RED WINES & GRAPES

"'Mr. Alakbarov, how much is the rent for this fantastic apartment?' 'Madam, this is the red wine aisle of the grocery store.'" – Fuad Alakbarov, Exodus

BONARDA

I DON'T KNOW WHAT IT is about Argentina and France's relationship, but there's something curious there. In my previous book, I wrote about how Malbec was deported from France to find a new home in Argentina. For those of you who haven't read it, I'll catch you up to speed.

Malbec was not growing well in France. Unsurprisingly, French winemakers started boxing it out in favor of hardier grapes. It wasn't until some Argentine winemakers came along that it got its second chance south of the equator. Fast forward a few decades, and now Malbec is thriving in Argentina.

But the story of Argentinian acquisitions doesn't stop there. It turns out Malbec wasn't the only wine grape who got the boot from the French. Douce Noir, the grape responsible for

Argentine Bonarda wine, joined the Argentinian ranks as well. Except the French legitimately banned Douce Noir from being grown. They just avoided Malbec. Regardless, we have Argentina to thank for yet another dynamic red wine. And I'm not mad about it.

Unlike Malbec, which is a straightforward wine with few variances in terms of flavor and body, Bonarda wears many hats. It can be found as a still, sparkling, rosé, or even white variety. You can grab a bottle with oak aging or without any at all. You can even confuse it with Bonarda Piemontese, the Italian wine that bears no relation to the Bonarda in Argentina. Talk about a one-man show! So if you're in the mood for a South American stunner, opt for Argentina's second-most popular red, Bonarda. I promise Malbec won't be mad.

THE TASTING

THE BOTTLE: *Durigutti Bonarda 2015. Mendoza, Argentina. $16.*

Word on the street is that Argentinian Bonarda tastes eerily like Merlot, just a more exotic-tasting version. And that's exactly what I'm getting from my first wafts of this Durigutti. There's raspberry, plum, freshly sharpened pencil, and a cedarwood-smelling spice. It's that last hit of woody spiciness that sets Bonarda apart.

In taste, it's much of the same. Raspberries, red plums, paprika, and hot rocks kick off the flavor show. This medium-bodied wonder carries with it a fairly robust tannin level. Luckily, there's an acidic edge to it for balance.

As you continue tasting, the pencil graphite and hot rock flavors fade into the background. And the paprika turns into a woody cedar note that lingers on the tip of the tongue. It's like drinking Syrah and Malbec's baby born in a bonfire. Spicy, juicy, cedary, and full of tannin. Bonarda has the same gumption as Malbec, yes, but they're two separate reds. Where Malbec is reserved and fruity, Bonarda is woody and spiced. Maybe France should send more of its rejects down to Argentina—they're producing some real powerhouses.

IN THE WILD

Argentinian Bonarda is the perfect complement to any outdoor cooking situation, especially a spit-roast. Any entrée that's been thoroughly given the spice rub treatment and set to linger over an open flame begs for a Bonarda. The deeply colored fruit coupled with the subtle paprika spice and cedar aftertaste brings out anything roasted over an open fire. Except for chestnuts; save those for Christmas and Zinfandel.

CARIGNAN

To find a French bottle, look in: the southern Rhône
(Côtes-du-Rhône), and Languedoc-Roussillon
(Corbières, Faugères, Minervois)

CARIGNAN HAS HAD A BIT of a past. I think of it as the troubled teenager of southern France. At times, you can see its potential. At others, you almost don't even want to bother with it. And this all started back in the 1980s.

A few decades ago, Carignan was planted all over the world: Rioja, Spain; Côte d'Azur, France; Chile, Italy, Morocco, and California, to name just a few. Winemakers loved it for its tendency to over-produce. The more wine you could make (albeit very bland ones at such high quantities), the more money you'd pocket. They extorted poor Carignan for quantity well throughout the 20th century. That is until the European Union offered winemakers subsidies for pulling up their vines and replacing them with "improved varieties" such as Grenache and Syrah.

Who knew monopolies, subsidies, and the government played such a role in winemaking? I certainly didn't, but those political actions served a pivotal role in the production of Carignan. What once was an over-produced workhorse has had to drastically rebrand as an ingredient in wines of quality. And it hasn't been easy.

Carignan takes a long time to ripen, necessitates a warm climate, and needs to be sprayed at a near-constant clip to prevent mildew and rot. Even then, it can still produce mediocre varietal wines. So it usually ends up in the mix of Côtes du Rhône blends. But sometimes, you can stumble on a single varietal bottle of Carignan that proves it has potential. Because this troubled teenager has a lot to go around. It just needs more time to grow into its true expression. I have no doubts that within the next few years, Carignan will finally get itself figured out.

THE TASTING

THE BOTTLE: *Domaine Lafage Tessellae Old Vines Carignan 2017. Côtes du Roussillon, France. $14.*

Despite its troubled past, Carignan is still a notable French wine. And that means tannin, acid, and under-ripe fruits. French reds are so predictable it hurts.

Quelle surprise, this bottle of Domaine Lafage fits the bill. Notes of raspberries, dark cherries, and cranberries lead you on nicely. If you didn't know any better, you'd think you were in for a pleasantly ripe, juicy tasting experience. *Wrong.*

Instead, there's under-ripe blackberry, medicinal cherry flavor, brown leather, slate, and dirty leaf flavors. There's zero evidence of oak, which shouldn't be a surprise—this bottle was aged in stainless steel tanks. And the tannins and acid are in classic French proportion: medium tannin, high acid.

As far as French reds go, Carignan is a perfect intermediary between the fuller-bodied Syrahs or Bordeauxes and the lighter, fruitier Beaujolaises. It's got all the seriousness of the former without all the pretense. Looks like Carignan has a place in the world after all.

IN THE WILD

Carignan is the wine you have when you want to be low-key impressive. You know you could easily go for a Barolo or a Bordeaux to give the impression that you're sophisticated, elegant, and have amazing taste. But those choices would be much too obvious. So, instead, you opt for another French variety.

Carignan isn't as big and bold as Bordeaux, but it's also not as casual as France's flirty Beaujolais. As a result, you trick everyone into thinking you're a true connoisseur. Offering a French red that few have heard of, a wine without widely known prestige, and yet with a profile similar to France's most esteemed reds? Yeah, people will buy into that. And now suddenly you're the wine-savvy one in the group. Congratulations on pulling a fast one! Carignan would be so proud.

CARMÉNÈRE

To find a French bottle, look in: Bordeaux (virtually extinct here)

REMEMBER WHEN I SAID THAT Argentina and France have an interesting relationship when it comes to wine grapes? Remember how France cast aside Malbec and Bonarda for not living up to expectations? And how Argentina adopted them, and now they're both thriving? Well, it would seem that Argentina isn't the only South American country benefitting from France's rejects. Carménère from Chile knows all about the French rejection, too.

Here's the thing: in the 1860s, phylloxera ruined wine. This teeny-tiny insect that feeds on grape roots destroyed an obscene amount of the wine crop in Europe. So much so that it looked like a death sentence for winemakers. Obviously, we know that never happened and Europe rebounded, since we all enjoy their bottles year-in, year-out. But this insect-ridden wipeout is the reason the French kicked Carménère out of Bordeaux.

After the phylloxera drama, the Bordelais decided "Eh, since the bug got rid of all the Carménère crop, we might as well replant with something hardier." So they did. Carménère was no more, and Merlot and Cab Sauv took its place. Luckily, the savvy winemakers down in Chile had already picked up vine cuttings for themselves, pre-bug.

Fast forward 134 years and Carménère became its own distinct entity, thriving in the warmer climate of Chile. Before 1994, the Carménère that grew in Chile was thought to be Merlot—but a smart scientist name Jean-Michel Boursiquot did some DNA testing and found that, aha!, Chile's vines were actually Carménère, not Merlot. Ever since, we've all been able to enjoy yet another Merlot-adjacent, luscious red wine that tastes as exotic as the culture it hails from. Trust me, Carménère is no run-of-the-mill medium-bodied red. It's savory, spicy, and sometimes even distinctly smoky. If there's one thing I've learned on my wine journey, it's that France's rejects shine in South America.

THE TASTING

THE BOTTLE: *Vendaval Reserva Carménère 2017. Colchagua, Chile. $15.*

The more wines I taste that resemble Merlot, whether in taste or genetics, the more I realize that Merlot is very appealing. It makes me wonder what happened to Miles in *Sideways* that made him hate it so much. Poor guy. Maybe he should try a Carménère and see how he feels after.

The varying scents of raspberry juice, blackberry, tobacco, and forest floor in this bottle should be enough to entice. Then again, I am partial to a tobacco-scented wine myself—very masculine and intriguing.

Luckily, the tobacco notes transfer over in flavor. The blackberry steps up first, followed by a triple berry jam flavor, and finishing with sweetly spicy tobacco. At first, the high alcohol content coupled with the tobacco flavor gives off an almost ash-like taste. Not exactly the manifestation I was hoping for, but luckily the subsequent sips prove to be much more balanced.

The smoky, spicy tobacco and the blended berry flavors balance each other out nicely, producing a clean, dry finish. It's not too full, not too light—a perfect middling body with flavor to match. The Vendaval Reserva is like drinking a Merlot after taking a puff from a cigar. And just like that, smoking cigars now has a perfect wine to go along with it.

IN THE WILD

Carménère is the true match for any cigar smoking sesh. It's dry, refined in flavor, sweetly smoky—everything you could need from a wine of this occasion. It's just as robust and bold as any Cabernet or Bordeaux blend. It brings the fruit of the Merlot necessary to offset the smoke. Yet it maintains a distinct level of body that neither fades into the background nor overpowers the cigars at hand. It's as close to a perfect pairing as one can get—Carménère and cigars. Open the humidor, crack open a bottle, and sit back and let the sophistication wash over you like liquid smoke.

LAMBRUSCO

SEEING AS HOW MY ENTRY-POINT to the wine world was $5 bottles of Barefoot Moscato, I'm never one to shy away from wines that people often sneer at. And Lambrusco has held the title for "Red Wines Worth a Sneer" since the 70s and 80s. The wine boom of the 70s brought forth some great wines and some... not-so-great wines. Exhibit A: the Riunite Lambrusco of 1981.

Riunite produced a cheap Lambrusco so teeth-achingly sweet and soda pop-esque, that people bought it up in droves. It was weird, unique, and ultracheap. Naturally, it became one of the top three imported wines in the USA back in 1981 (the other two being, get this, other brands of Lambrusco). But, like all unusual, not-actually-good food and drink ideas, it fell to a level so low that people could only do one thing: sneer.

Now, after the Riunite Ruining of the 80s, Lambrusco still can't seem to claw its way out. It's not like it hasn't tried. Production has improved dramatically in quality; they've introduced the Charmat fermentation method used with Prosecco to up the class factor, and they're producing a variety of styles and sweetness levels—because no one wants to try syrupy wine soda more than once.

So, if you're bored one day and are itching to watch a classic John Hughes movie, you might as well find an adventurous Lambrusco to go with it. It's kitschy enough, you just might love it.

THE TASTING

THE BOTTLE: *Medici Ermete I Quercioli Lambrusco Reggiano Dolce. Emilia-Romagna, Italy. $11.*

As I said, I'm not above a sweet wine, even one whose reputation precedes it. Wanting to dive in at the deep end, I chose a Lambrusco Dolce—the sweetest variety you can get. I figured, if I hate it, I know there's a drier variety available. But I was feeling adventurous and wanted to see what all the chatter was about.

Since people often chill Lambrusco, I went ahead and popped it in the fridge before tasting. In retrospect, I probably shouldn't have. Trying to smell or taste anything distinct, flavor-wise, was not in the realm of possibility for at least 15-20 minutes. But once it approached room temperature, I got my opportunity.

This bottle smelled like honey and Welch's sparkling red grape juice. And it tasted like artificial blackberry syrup, honey, and Welch's sparkling red grape juice. Not a very complex wine, but I guess the dolce variety masks all the flavor opportunities with a thick layer of sweetness.

Regardless, the bubbles are persistent and delicately frothy. And that acidity from the Welch's sensation is a nostalgic comfort, too. This bottle of Lambrusco Dolce is like biting into a fruity truffle. The outside is thickly coated in berry-flavored syrup and honey, but when you bite into it, the acidic sparkling grape juice flavor bursts forward. It's not a lot, and it's not in contention for any accolades, but it's a sweet treat.

IN THE WILD

Lambrusco Dolce is the wine you drink when you want a dessert wine, but you're not ready to commit to a port or a sherry. The Lambrusco is less intimidating, so it's a good gateway wine between the dry and the dessert. Kind of like a red version of Moscato. A very approachable, entry-level, red kind of somethin' to mix up the monotony of tannins and citrusy acid.

Although, should you want something less sweet but just as unique, a dry or off-dry variety would pair perfectly with any nostalgic rendezvous. Be it your favorite movie from your childhood, a gathering of old friends (who don't mind off-beat wines), or a sneaky way to drink at a kid's birthday party, Lambrusco can up your kitsch level in a snap. It might not be chic and sophisticated, but at least it's fun. Cheers to Lambrusco for keeping us all forever young.

MENCÍA

MENCÍA IS ONE OF THOSE wines that makes it easy to dabble in new territories. More often than not, most of us stick to the wines we know, the regions we're comfortable with, and leave it at that. We don't know what other varietals taste like, nor do we know what's comparable to the wines we already like. Is there another wine that's like Pinot Noir that you'll love? Is there an alternative for Cabernet Franc? Sauvignon Blanc? The list goes on and on—although we've already learned that Grüner Veltliner is coming for you, Sauv Blanc. But as for Mencía, it's a red that all Cab Franc lovers should pay more attention to.

The best part about Mencía is it's not complicated. You can only get a bottle from Spain. Okay, technically, 1% of the world's Mencía grapes are grown in Portugal, but that's barely worth noting. Because of its regional exclusivity, the flavor differences are minimal. Although if you get a bottle from Ribera Scara, there's a bit of deviation depending on which slope your vineyard sits on. No, seriously—it supposedly makes a difference.

Now this is where Cab Franc lovers need to perk their ears up. All the dark fruit, earthy, and sometimes vegetal flavors you love can also be found in a bottle of Mencía. Just in lesser intensities. It could be equally good, could be disappointing; but you won't know if Mencía is a worthwhile tangent unless you try. Who knows? Maybe for those who don't love a traditional Cab Franc, Mencía's more subtle, earthy notes make it a palatable addition to their rotation of reds. Either way, Spain offers a moody red that's worth a tasting trip.

THE TASTING

THE BOTTLE: *Marqués de Toro Finca La Moura Mencía 2012. Castilla y León, Spain. $12.*

As promised, this bottle of Marqués de Toro brings the fruit and earth right off the bat. You've got cherry, pomegranate, black licorice, and moss hitting the nose all at once. It's like taking a huge whiff of Pinot Noir while you're standing in the middle of the woods. Although, if you can relate to that, I've got some questions.

The tasting itself is just as earthy as the aroma. The flavors resemble a berry-flavored lozenge that rolled around in the spice cabinet (and then in the dirt), with a hint of crushed gravel, while black licorice hides in the back. The berry flavors of cherry mixed with raspberry spar with the spices, both the baking and Italian variety. Then there's the essence of dirt and crushed gravel to join the party.

With such a red-fruity kind of wine, you can expect the acidity to be fairly high. In fact, the acid and potent cherry flavors lead you to believe the wine is lighter in body than it is. One look at the legs in your glass, and you realize your error in judgment. That is, if the tannins don't get to you first.

Overall, Mencía lives up to its promise. And for someone who isn't fond of Cab Franc, I'd happily have another bottle of Mencía when offered. It's fruity, earthy, and reminds me of foliage in the best way. Dare I say, it's a perfect wine to enjoy in the forest while foraging (just kidding; you'd break your glass or get a bug in it). Maybe a more civilized forest adventure would be a better fit.

IN THE WILD

Mencía is the wine you take to a lake house or, God forbid, camping in the crisp fall season. The most obvious reason is that you need some booze to both warm you up and to pacify any non-nature lovers (hello, me). Beyond the necessities, Mencía's flavor is cut out for the job. The tart, yet deep red berry flavors taste forest-foraged, with the hints of dried herbs and spices, crushed gravel, and earthy flavors to round out the "Into the Woods" tasting experience. It's not too bright, not too fruity— just earthy and rugged enough to pair perfectly with a lurking fall night amidst the chilly fog, pitch-black trees, and humming crickets.

MOURVÈDRE

To find a French bottle, look in: the southern Rhône (Châteauneuf-du-Pape, Gigondas, Vacqueyras, Rasteau, Côtes-du-Rhône) and Languedoc-Roussillon (Corbières, Faugères, Fitou, Minervois)

THIS DARK-SKINNED VARIETY IS KNOWN by three names: Mourvèdre in France, Monastrell in Spain, and Mataro in Australia and the USA. As frustrating as that may be (why not just pick one, you guys?), stumbling upon a bottle is much easier. Remember the ever-popular Rhône/GSM blends from my first book? Allow me to re-introduce you to the "M," my friend.

One of the three major grapes in Châteauneuf-du-Pape wines, Mourvèdre has been stunning the wine world for centuries. With its dark, fruity, smoky, and sometimes even meaty flavors, this grape brings serious depth. Which makes it an ideal blending partner in red wine blends around the world. What would a red blend be without a little smoky, tannic depth? Juice, that's what.

But even outside of blends, Mourvèdre can be a serious single-varietal contender. Granted, this grape is a notoriously late bloomer and sometimes won't produce any quality grapes for years after it's first planted. So, patience on the winegrowers' behalf is a must for cranking out high-quality single-varietal bottles. But it's worth it for a chance to sample Big M on its own.

If one chooses a French Mourvèdre, expect more meat, herbs, and earth flavors. Fruit-forward has never been much of France's vibe. But Spanish Monastrell, on the other hand, is full of dark juicy fruits like blackberry and plum. And the adventurers among us who opt for the less popular Australian or American Mataro should be ready to welcome a richer and more fruit-driven variety—even more so than its Mediterranean counterparts.

No matter where you sample, expect depth, tannins, and a voluptuous full-bodied affair. Maybe even buckle yourself in with a seatbelt, because Mourvèdre is a force to be reckoned with.

THE TASTING

THE BOTTLE: *Bodegas Olivares Altos de la Hoya Monastrell 2017. Jumilla, Spain. $12.*

From my cursory Google searches, French Mourvèdre is much more expensive than Spanish Monastrell. So, I figured I would stay true to my budget and my fellow budgeteers and went for a Monastrell. Seeing as how this grape originated in Spain, you can't really go wrong here.

Despite a cost of only $12, the Olivares brings all the classic flavors, plus a heavy hand of oak with blackberries, leather, vanilla, cigar box, and peppercorns. Being a major oak fan, I am all for the multi-faceted oak players here. And there's certainly enough room for them, seeing as the wine's texture is soft and full-bodied. Any other lighter-bodied wine wouldn't do the flavor profile justice. But this Olivares is plush and merits a broad range of flavor.

Now, Mourvèdre (and its regional synonyms) are notorious for high tannins. This bottle of Olivares has them, but they're diffused and soft—nothing like the grippy variety often associated with Bordeaux blends or Syrah. Instead, it makes for a lusciously mellow tasting experience, and I am here for it.

Monastrell tastes like a wine that you've had for years and just blew the dust off. It's got a masculine, antique edge with the dark fruit, cigar box, and leather notes. A flavor profile that's perfect for old blues records.

IN THE WILD

Spanish Monastrell is the penultimate wine for a soulful kickback. You've got the classics present: suede loafers, B.B. King and Etta James, fresh-cut cigars in the humidor, and all your oldest friends under one roof. It's been so long since you've all been together, there's hardly any time for small talk. Yet you know the next few hours will fly by quickly amidst deep conversations and never-empty drinks. While it's easy to opt for a whiskey or even a cognac during times like these, a Monastrell is an equally suave fit for the occasion. With a plush mouthfeel and smooth structure, it's an elegant red wine with all the soul of barrel-aged whiskey.

NERO D'AVOLA

NERO D'AVOLA IS SICILY'S BABY, hands-down. And that's saying something, considering this Mediterranean island has been producing wines of all styles for 3,000 years and counting. So, if you've yet to come across a bottle of Nero, consider this a friendly-yet-necessary introduction.

Once upon a time, in the 20th century, Nero d'Avola was only used as a blending grape. Its dark hue and bold fruit flavors were often used to bolster weak blends. But then, right around the birth of the millennials, Nero d'Avola had a rebirth of its own.

Winemakers started to appreciate all that this dark-skinned grape offered (the color is almost black, hence the name, as "nero" is Italian for black). Thanks to a handful of brave and persistent Sicilian producers, Nero d'Avola started to shine as a single-varietal wine.

Luckily for wine drinkers everywhere, we all have another option when choosing a fuller-bodied red. Maybe your Syrah is becoming a bit too peppery or unforgiving with its unripe fruit flavor. Or maybe you find yourself bored with the same old Cab Sauv and want something slightly different. Cue Nero.

Fans of Syrah or Cabernet Sauvignon can easily gravitate towards Nero d'Avola. The bold fruit is there, the tannin and acid are there (in perfect harmony, I might add), and the body is round and full. Everything you love in your go-tos is present in Sicily's finest. Nero's just presented in a more plush package. Plus, it's easy to find a delicious and high-quality bottle for less than $20. But why take my word for it? Let's give Nero a taste, and see, yet again, how Italy makes wow-worthy wines without damaging our wallets.

THE TASTING

THE BOTTLE: *Tasca d'Almerita Lamuri Nero d'Avola 2016. Sicily, Italy. $17.*

Nero d'Avola comes in two varieties: the young, zippy, and herbal kind with little to no oak; and the opulent, dark fruit, sometimes chocolatey kind with ample evidence of oak. I'm led to believe that this bottle lies curiously in-between.

Tasca d'Almerita Lamuri is full of cherry juice, olive, and spice on the nose in a way that isn't affronting. One point for the young, zippy variety. But the taste muddies the water a bit.

Tart cherry, blueberry, violet, and a racing stripe of graphite make the differences between both faces of Nero even harder to distinguish. Mostly because the cherry flavor morphs from tart to soft black cherry. Then the blueberry and graphite sneak their way in. But wait, is that chewing tobacco I taste? Another wrench in the flavor department! Maybe the structure will give me the direction I need.

This Tasca is full-bodied. There are no two ways about it. The legs are insane and the thickness coats your mouth way more than I had expected. In terms of tannin/acid balance, the tannins are more powerful than the acidity, but they're very smooth and palatable. This leads me to believe that this bottle of Nero d'Avola leans more towards the more opulent, dark fruit end of the spectrum. No complaints here.

It has such a soft, luscious fruit and floral flavor that it feels like licking velvet: the height of opulence and richness. Nero, you're a stunner.

IN THE WILD

Nero d'Avola is the Dita Von Teese of wines, always donning her signature red lip, tightly wound corset, and voluminous wavy curls. She's both inviting yet dominant, ensuring that her audience stays captive. Nero's tart cherry—iconically red—and subtle floral notes exude confident femininity while the graphite edge draws the line between flavorful lust and constraint. It's a dance, a production, a display of luscious, tantalizing power and seduction. All tightly wound within the bounds of endless ruby velvet. If you want a hypnotic dance masquerading as a wine, Nero's your lady.

PETITE SIRAH

BEFORE YOU ASK, NO, PETITE Sirah is not a cuter, tinier version of Syrah/Shiraz. The grapes are indeed related, but so are Cabernet Sauvignon and Sauvignon Blanc. And we all know those two are clearly not flavor twins. The same goes for Petite Sirah and Syrah. Sure, they're both red varietals and share a genetic thread, but that's where the similarities end. Now that we've cleared up any confusion, let's talk about California's other exclusive-majority red wine contribution (next to Zinfandel, of course).

Petite Sirah is a true underdog. Having been a California native since the late 1800s, you'd think it would be wildly popular in the USA, much like Zinfandel and oaky Chardonnay.

Or that it'd be given respect for its high-quality production. But it's been quite the opposite experience for our little Petite.

Bearing resemblance to a noble grape like Syrah, but not being a carbon-copy in structure and flavor, has caused wine snobs across the globe to snub it as a lesser-than wine. They say it's not established enough, which honestly sounds more like a "them problem" than a Petite Sirah problem. Petite's been around longer than all of us—what do you mean not *established* enough?

Their judgment error aside, wine lovers and growers everywhere are on a mission to get this unique little grape "established" once and for all (since 200+ years of production doesn't seem to be enough). There's even a campaign lovingly called "P.S. I Love You" advocating for this long-standing grape. But all of that means nothing if you haven't met P.S. yourself.

Zinfandel lovers will enjoy it; Syrah lovers will enjoy it; heck, even Cabernet lovers will enjoy it. In structure and flavor, Petite Sirah is the complete, silky package. Just don't expect a petite tasting experience.

THE TASTING

THE BOTTLE: *Field Recordings Pets 2018. Paso Robles, CA. $18.*

Truth be told, there are subtle yet noticeable flavor variations in a bottle of Petite depending on the region you purchase from—even within California. But what seems to be consistent across the board are flavors of blueberry, chocolate, plum, and even black pepper. This bottle from Field Recordings isn't far off the mark.

With scents of blueberry sauce, raspberry, and chocolate shavings, I'm intrigued. Occasionally, tasting notes will offer chocolate as a suggestion. And every time, I always think "good one, guys." Never have I ever tasted, let alone smelled, chocolate in a dry wine until now. And I'm quickly becoming a fan.

The flavor is an even match: blueberry, milk chocolate truffle with raspberry filling, and 1/16 teaspoon of black pepper. Yes, the specific amount of pepper is required, because my version of a pinch is probably not your version of a pinch and I wanted to be *precise*.

This bottle is an absolute delight. The tannins are sky-high, yes, but the flavor and acid are so smooth, it's hardly a bother. If the tannins were less dominant, this would taste like the driest dessert wine ever. It's practically a chocolaterie in a glass, that's how rich it is. The body is equally decadent. It's leggy, full, and as close to molasses as wine could probably get. Luckily, the tannin and tightly zipped acidity keep it from straying off the "true wine" path.

This bottle from Field Recordings is decadent and luscious without bearing any residual sweetness, which, to me, is a fascinating feat. Think cocoa powder mixed with macerated blueberries and raspberries—dessert-like, but not sugary. Add in the 1/16 teaspoon of black pepper and you've got an amazing flavor experience. One deserving of an equally decadent setting.

IN THE WILD

Petite Sirah from the central coast of California is the quintessential Valentine's Day wine. Especially if your valentine ranks wine and chocolate equally as their ultimate comforts. Petite Sirah (from Paso Robles, especially) is decadent, rich, and gives off the feeling of dessert without all the added sugar. Which means the only sugar provided will be from you to yours. The rest of us will have to rely on Petite Sirah's chocolatey lovin'.

PINOTAGE

I REMEMBER MY FIRST PINOTAGE like it was yesterday. Despite sounding like a woman who's greying from accumulated age and wisdom, it's true. The first time I had ever heard of the varietally named wine and my first taste were within minutes of each other. Probably for the best—the longer I have to research something, the higher my expectations grow. But with Pinotage, I had none, and ironically, I'll always fondly remember that first encounter.

The impression was immediate. One whiff of the stuff and I was blown away. Here before me was a wine that smelled (and tasted) perplexingly like smoked brisket and cherry juice. Like the Albariño and its salty notes, I wasn't sure I would ever come across a meat-flavored wine. But here, staring me in the face, was a glass emitting flavors that I assumed were just a fantasy, anomaly, or stretch of the sensory imagination. And I *loved it.*

Ever since, I've been hunting for a similar bottle. Leave it to me to be so bowled over by a flavor experience that I forget to get the pertinent information about the bottle. But even so, finding another identical glass would be easier said than done—Pinotage is wildly unpredictable.

Sure, it's known for its juicy fruit flavors, but those can range from light and predominantly red-flavored to dense and dark fruit-flavored. And, yes, a Pinotage can give off strong smoky bacon (or brisket) notes, but sometimes it's subtle and easily overpowered by licorice or tar flavors. The range is appealing to many, but it also serves as an unpredictable thicket for those trying to recreate a flavor experience.

Still, Pinotage is such a fun excursion that I'll never be deterred. After all, Pinotage completely changed the way I looked at the flavor possibilities of a bottle of red. What Albariño did for me with white wines, Pinotage did for the reds. So, my fellow salty, smoky, savory lovers, do yourself a favor and get to know South Africa's red gem. I can guarantee you'll be best friends in no time.

THE TASTING

THE BOTTLE: *Robertson Winery Pinotage 2018. Western Cape, South Africa. $11.*

This bottle did not come easily to me. As I said, I have been on the hunt to recreate my very first Pinotage flavor experience for years. This tasting was no exception. I pored through Vivino tasting notes, pages of search results, and scoured inventories of wine stores who would ship to me without forcing me to take out a personal loan to pay for it. In terms of a matching flavor profile, this bottle was the second closest (the first being the 2017 vintage, but that was nowhere to be found). So, unlike my first whimsical encounter, my expectations this time around were astronomical.

I tentatively took a sniff. Not an identical match, but there were similarities. Initially, there was a strong bouquet of brown leather school bus seats, cherries, and raspberries. But after resting the wine in the glass for a few minutes, I smelled it. The smell that brought me back to my first dalliance: mesquite smoke. It wasn't exactly brisket, but it was close. Besides, all I really wanted was another meaty wine. I was salivating at the thought that I might get my wish. I just didn't expect it to be delivered in such an eccentric way.

The Robertson of 2018 tastes like you just snapped in a cherry-and-strawberry-flavored retainer on the roof of your mouth. Never mind the old brown leather flavors circulating throughout the remaining crevices. Brown leather that deliciously transforms into smoky mesquite, that is. Heaven.

The pungent red fruits and smoky, leathery, meaty flavors are all wrapped up in a full body with low acidity and smooth tannins bearing a striking resemblance to liquid smoke. The texture is so smooth, one might dare to call it creamy. It's a jarringly calm wine for such big flavors. And I can't say that I'm disappointed, despite my high expectations.

There's a reason Pinotage rhymes with mirage—the flavors ebb and flow and you never know what you're going to get and at what level of intensity. Sometimes there's a lot of meat flavor, other times there's hardly any. Sometimes you get soft fruit flavor, other times it'll punch you right in the face. This bottle falls somewhere in between with a texture that is silky and divine. But that liquid smoke demands a southern-style caliber of respect that anyone can appreciate.

IN THE WILD

Pinotage is that commanding old southern man, with a perfectly groomed salt and pepper mustache, a low southern drawl, and a withering stare. Think Sam Elliott's looks and Clint Eastwood's demeanor. This man commands every room, if not for the sole reason that there's a rifle stashed somewhere in his house. He's got a hard demeanor, but it's softened by his pride and joys: his daughters. The love he has for his always-my-baby girls makes him human and approachable.

It's the same way for a Pinotage. The leather, smoky, mesquite flavors are gentlemanly southern comfort and, at times, prove unyielding. But even the sternest Pinotages have their soft spots: their ripe red fruit flavor that has the potential to coat the entire upper half of your mouth. The balance of flavor will shift depending on its mood, but all in all, a Pinotage will never change its character. Much like a Clint Eastwood-type father from the south. It may not suit everyone, but you'll never forget your first encounter.

PORTUGUESE RED BLEND

I'LL BE HONEST. FOR THE longest time, I had always avoided "red blends" when buying wine. Why? Because it seemed like a copout. To me, if a wine was any good, then it could stand on its own as a single varietal. I erroneously assumed that the blends were hiding something: subpar wines. But after diving into Côtes du Rhône blends in *From Cabernet to Zinfandel*, I saw the error of my ways. Not only that, but I learned that other regions outside of France and the United States are producing enticing red blends of their own. This time around, it's Portugal.

Normally, when people think of Portuguese wines, they think of two: Port (duh) and Vinho Verde. I'd argue that few other wines come to mind when Spain's neighbor is brought up. I can't say I blame anyone. Port has been around for a zillion years, hiding out in the libraries and cellars of posh dignitaries and anyone with war stories and gray hair. And Vinho Verde is yet another crisp, dry white wine that can swap in for almost any other crisp, dry white wine. But other than that, Portugal rarely comes up. Probably because this elusive wine region has been producing dry red wines on the down-low in quiet solitude. Before the 2000s, hardly anyone except for the Portuguese was hip to their dry red wine offerings. But eventually, all wines creep into the global network. Even if it takes 20+ years.

Now, the time has come for Portugal to rev up the red blend scene. And, boy, have they delivered. The variety of red blends from the Douro alone can range from light and fruity to dark and dense (and everywhere in between). Never mind that the Dão, Lisbon, Alentejo, Beira, and Tejo regions have their own crave-worthy contributions. If there's one thing I've learned from all my tastings so far (and, clearly, I've learned a lot), it's that the wines you're most likely to snub are the ones that are full of the best surprises. First Zinfandel, now regional red blends—I'm sorry I ever doubted you.

THE TASTING

THE BOTTLE: *Casa Santos Lima Lisboa Colossal Reserva 2015. Lisboa, Portugal. $10.*

Now any wine termed 'Colossal' is highly unlikely to wind up being light and fruity. So, I'm going to assert right off the bat that this Lisbon red blend will be a full-bodied treat. With aromas of plum, raspberry sauce, red rose, and allspice, it's bringing forth what's becoming my favorite thing about blends: the sensory smorgasbord.

But does it live up to its name in taste? The combination of blackberry, plums, dried herbs, black licorice, and a hint of cedary vanilla conclusively point to *yes*. The acid, tannins, and herb and spice flavors make for a gigantic mouthful. None of the elements at play are overt or overpowering the other. It's just the combo of all three at once that makes for a more impactful sensation. But that's just the second act.

The dark fruit flavors of blackberry and plum coat your tongue first, laying down a full-bodied flavor foundation. Then comes the herby, anise-sprinkled grip of tannins and acid that take over your whole mouth. It has the same sensation as taking a shot of chilled (high quality—no Burnett's, please) vodka. The chill coats your tongue, while the astringency follows up the rear. Same one-two punch going on here. First the fruit, then the astringent tannins.

I have to hand it to Portugal. Their red blends lack nothing when compared to a French variety. The Colossal is tightly wound, full of dark fruit (while not being overtly juicy), and laced with herbs and spices. If it's the exotic nuance you're looking for in red blends, give ol' Lisbon a try. They'll leave nothing on the table but a lasting impression.

IN THE WILD

A Portuguese red blend, especially one from Lisbon, is the wine you grab when you've had it up to here. Lord help you—if one more person nags you, refuses to listen, or just flat out rubs you the wrong way, you're gonna lose it. Unless you pour yourself a red blend from Lisbon. The dark fruits immediately begin soothing by delivering juicy comfort. But the spices, herbs, and tightly wound structure mirror your riled-up state, reminding you that you have every right to be upset. It's not trying to pacify; it's trying to keep you from boiling over. Keep on sipping—the finish is long enough to endure whatever it is you're going through. Eventually, the alcohol will kick in and the fruity warmth will make you realize that tomorrow's another day. And if not, you always have the rest of the bottle... right?

VALPOLICELLA BLEND

CAN WE ALL FINALLY ADMIT that Italy has achieved perfect balance in their wines? I've yet to come across a bottle that can't equally be enjoyed as a standalone or with a full-on Italian feast. And to me, that's impressive. So often we come across "either-or" bottles, and how bottles fall into either category can change from one person to the next. But Valpolicella? This blended beauty can spectacularly do both and, better yet, comes in four different flavor tiers (and price points).

At one end of the spectrum, you have standard Valpolicella—a bright, tangy, light-bodied wine full of sour cherry notes. It's casual, fruity, and can even benefit from a slight chill on the bottle. Consider this your entry-level variety.

Next up, you have Valpolicella Ripasso. At this tier, you get a richer, more concentrated flavor, and a medium to full-bodied variety. It's soft, elegant, and the more business- or romantic-casual of the four. Naturally, it's a step-up in price from the standard Valpolicella.

The upper echelon of dry Valpolicella varieties is Amarone. It's aged for a minimum of two years (usually for five) and produces a wine that has such dynamic and rich flavors, it's comparable to a dessert wine in impact. In fact, you can easily age a bottle of Amarone for 10-20 years and have it still be amazing. Expect to spend half a century note on a bottle, though.

Finally, there's Recioto—the most expensive and the only dessert variety of the four. Made in a similar process to Amarone, and therefore packs an equal amount of flavor, it's altered to maintain some of the grape's residual sugars. You can also cellar Recioto for a *long* time—like 20-30 years, long. And word on the street is that Recioto is a fire combination with dark chocolate, so let's all keep that in mind.

Still don't believe in Italian wines being the pinnacle of balance and variety? Fine; let's open a bottle of Valpolicella and have a taste for ourselves.

THE TASTING

THE BOTTLE: *Italo Cescon Ca'della Scala Mezzopiano Valpolicella Ripasso Superiore 2016. Veneto, Italy. $19.*

Since I'm a glutton for rich Italian flavors, wine included, I went with the Ripasso. And at a price point of $19, I have to say this bottle exceeded my expectations across the board.

First up: the aromas. Tart cherry, vanilla, dried herbs, and a new leather jacket all mingle together to make an intriguing, dominant first impression. If anyone can make a new leather jacket work for it, it's an Italian red.

The taste is *chef's kiss*. Pomegranate juice, vanilla, cedar, and a hint of dark chocolate and coffee-ground flavor all blend in a wildly rustic way. It's oaky, fruity, cedary, and acidic as all get out, but it works! The result is a perfect Italian demonstration of what a little bit of oak can do for a wine's flavor profile. You go from vanilla, to cedary, fresh sharpened pencil, to a dark chocolate and coffee amalgamation. And yet nothing about it tastes out of place.

Seeing as how this is a 2016 bottle, I'm thrilled with what a little amount of age has done for the tasting experience. The flavors are more settled—not bouncing around your mouth, as a younger wine would. Instead, the flavors are collected and concentrated and, as a result, the bottle tastes much more mature in its presentation.

Valpolicella is a fantastic wine to bring out for any Italian dinner without the cliche of reaching for the ever-impressive Barolo or deferring to the common centerpiece of Chianti. It's a lovely, age-worthy middle ground that's both flavorful and fruity and still mature in its composure.

IN THE WILD

Valpolicella Ripasso is the "first date with Italian food" wine. Unlike the 'value level' of a standard Valpolicella, this higher-class designation will impress without making you broke in the process (let's be honest, it's a first date—save the high-priced wines for a bigger commitment). The fruitiness is inviting, the oaky presence is rich, and the whole sensory experience screams "rich and soft"—a perfect balance for an immaculate first impression. Throw on some of Frank Sinatra's best odes to Italy and opt for a dinner with mushrooms or savory umami flavors, and you've got yourself a locked-in second date, my friend.

NOTES FROM THE OTHER SIDE

(of 25 more bottles)

DABBLING IN THE WORLD OF wine can lead you anywhere. You could find a bottle that changes everything for you, thanks to its supreme quality or eye-opening flavor. You can find new favorites from varieties you never would've noticed otherwise. You can open yourself up to the entire world, with each country offering you a new perspective on what wine can be. Or you can find it all a frustrating charade and relegate wine to an alcoholic beverage and nothing more. Totally up to you. Although, if it's the last option, then I've done a terrible job at sharing my love of wine with you.

For me, it's been a little of each so far (the last option being the reason I almost gave up on the stuff altogether). In my first book, *From Cabernet to Zinfandel*, I learned to reconcile my preconceived notions by giving each wine a fair chance. And in doing so, I found my new favorite holiday wine, my go-to September white, and realized that Sauvignon Blanc and I will always have a rocky relationship. This time around, my eyes have been opened. Two books and 50 wines later, I now know that...

AROMATIC WINES ARE ALIVE AND WELL.

I don't think we ever have to worry about Gewürztraminer going out of style. It's ridiculous, exotic, and terribly fun to say out loud. Plus, today's ever-elevating wine standards make it more difficult to find a shoddy bottle than an excellent one (I'll drink to that).

Even more than the big G, there are other aromatics whose intense floral, citrus, or herby aromas make for an intoxicating experience. Viognier and her quintessentially feminine, posh notes. Riesling and its mandarin orange sweetness, making a name for itself by straddling both sides of the dry-sweet spectrum. And Torrontés, the hibachi grill of wines, putting on a show one spark at a time. There aren't many of them in the aromatic bunch, but boy do they all pack a punch.

THE WORLD OF REDS CAN DELIVER BOTH FEMININE AND MASCULINE NOTES.

White wines are more notorious for their feminine, floral notes. And reds can exhibit notes of leather or tobacco—arguably masculine flavors. But can either do both? Turns out, the often-monotonous world of reds can.

Try a Beaujolais and tell me it's not pretty, floral, and feminine. When I tasted it for the first time in *From Cabernet to Zinfandel,* I was shell-shocked. I never expected to encounter a red that was flirty and femme. And then I sat down with a Carménère and tasted quite the opposite—a cigar stubbed out in a glass of Merlot. I had found the masculine counterpart in the red world. Anyone can drink any wine they like, but let's be honest. Sometimes you want a bottle of flirty fun. And sometimes you want a husky, smoky bottle. Luckily for us, there's a red for both.

CRÉMANT IS AS CLOSE TO CUSTOMIZED BUBBLES AS YOU CAN GET.

Champagne is hard to stretch. It's always made from predominantly Chardonnay grapes and, as such, the flavors you'll encounter aren't all that unique from one bottle to the next. The boundary lines are drawn, and there's no getting around it. Unless you opt for Champagne's cousin, Crémant.

With nine different regional variations and a whole slew of different grapes that are eligible, Crémant is ideal for the Champagne savant who wants more variation. Don't like bubblies from Alsace? Try Limoux. Or Jura. Or the Loire. Or Burgundy. Try them all! The odds of you finding a French bubbly that speaks to your unique palate are much higher with Crémant than with Champagne. For those who can't be tamed, Crémant is a godsend.

RED BLENDS ARE LIKE A BOX OF CHOCOLATES – YOU NEVER KNOW WHAT YOU'RE GONNA GET.

Is the famous "box of chocolates" quote trite? Absolutely. Is it still applicable? Always. And with red blends, it hits the nail on the head.

Red blends sound vague because they *are* vague. They can be made from any domestic grape varieties and in varying amounts. Even red blends from the same state can taste different from one to the next. Throw in multiple countries, dozens of more grapes, and varying percentages, and you've got yourself a crapshoot! If you're ever in the mood for mystery or a frustrating and fascinating blind tasting with friends, the red blends are where it's at.

SAVORY WINES ARE A MUST-TRY IN EVERY WINE LOVER'S LIFE.

The two wines that changed the way I look at wine are Albariño and Pinotage. Both for the same reason: they defied my flavor expectations. Normally when drinking wine, your expectations in the flavor department are relatively limited. It's made from a fruit, so you expect fruity flavors. The fact that it's a plant opens the doors for plant-adjacent flavors. Throw the juice in an oak barrel, and you've got oaky flavors. There always seemed to be a defense for any flavor I found in my wines. Until I tried the flavor-defiers.

Albariño showed me what saltwater proximity can do for a wine's flavor in the most dramatically saline package I could imagine. And Pinotage? There's no logical reason for a wine to exhibit smoked meat flavors, and yet, there they were. Both savory, both wonderful. In fact, I wouldn't love the adventure of wine-tasting nearly as much if I hadn't encountered these two anomalies early on. Savory wines are intriguing—a detour worth making at least twice in your life. You know, one for the reds and one for the whites. And if you get hooked on the savory flavors like me, there are many more in your future.

ITALY MAKES THE MOST DIVERSIFIED HIGH-QUALITY WINES (IN MY HUMBLE OPINION).

France and California (Napa, specifically) always seem to get the gold medals for best in show. Something about their high-quality wines, or whatever. Maybe one day I'll understand what everyone's talking about. You know, drink the Kool-Aid and be able to regurgitate the fuss back to you. But I'll be honest, I'd rather gauge quality based on my own priorities when sitting down with a glass of wine. Flavor integrity and balance are the two key players for me, and no one seems to do it better than Italy.

Shea, what in God's name is flavor integrity? Did you just make up yet another inane wine term? Yes, yes, I did. To me, flavor integrity is how accurately flavors come forth when you taste. You can easily pick them out. They're distinct without seeming artificial or out of place. And when a bottle ages, the flavors taste refined and deeper. It's akin to braising a chicken in chicken broth. When it's done, that chicken flavor is amplified. The same can be said for a bottle of aged wine. After a few years, the flavors are deeper and more mature. A good Italian bottle brings that kind of flavor. And it's all in sync. Balance and flavor integrity—Italy's specialties.

PRICE POINT MATTERS, BUT MORE DOESN'T ALWAYS EQUAL BETTER.

Now, this isn't an exact science, but generally, any wine under $10 or over $50 is a gamble. On the pricier side, spending over $50 will rarely buy you a better tasting experience than what you can find in the $20-30 range. And on the cheaper side, spending less than $10 rarely gets you very far in terms of quality (emphasis on usually; I've found a couple of bottles for $9 that were tasty and balanced). That "happy medium" price point varies across the different varietals, but $15-20 seems to be the universal sweet spot.

It's safe to say that even after 50 wines, my learning hasn't stopped. I thought for sure that this time around it would be more of the same. That nothing groundbreaking was up for discovery. But I was wrong. As I have been many times along this journey. But the truth is, wine doesn't care. You can't mess up with wine; its sole purpose is to offer you more. Whether that's more flavor, perspective, cultural awareness, or just a toasty buzz, it will always be there to provide.

Now, it would be easy for me to set up camp here among the underrated varietals and be content. After all, who needs over 50 wines under their belt to function in society? But that's not what this journey is about. It's about discovery. It's about flavor exploration, taste refinement (my own), and embracing all the beautiful pockets of the world that contribute to the winemaking industry. So, I'm moving onwards. And this time, I'm bringing more unique varieties into the mix. Think Hungarian reds, Croatian whites, and a fun little Spanish wine called Bobal, to name a few. I hope you'll join me—it'll be the most exotic chapter yet. Until next time—cheers!

A SIMPLE FAVOR

Starring: Blake Lively, Anna Kendrick, and Your Honest Opinion

LET ME START BY THANKING you tremendously for taking the time to read *From Albariño to Torrontés*. I hope you laughed, learned, and had a blast in a glass learning about the world's most underrated wines. I can't wait to share even more niche and unique wines with you in book three!   That means more wines, more personalities, and more ways to fit the wines of the world into your fabulous life.

But before we dive into another installment of 25 more wines, I have a simple favor to ask. If you'd be so kind, I'd love it if you would post a review of *From Albariño to Torrontés*. Whether you loved it, hated it, or landed somewhere in between,

I'd love to hear your feedback. Reviews are hard to come by for lesser known authors and you, the reader, have the power to make or break a book. It doesn't have to be lengthy, or even a full sentence, just an honest opinion from you would mean the world.

If you can spare the time, head right over to my book's page on Amazon and drop a quick review. You'll be my new hero (even if you hated every last page of it).

Thank you again for spending time with me and my wine-fueled labor of love. I'll see you again for book number three.

In good wines and bad,
Shea

COMING SOON

FROM

Aglianico

TO

Rkatsiteli

FLAVORS, PAIRINGS, AND
PERSONALITIES OF THE WORLD'S
MOST UNIQUE WINES

SHEA SANDERSON